SOCIAL CHANGE IN THE LAW OF TRUSTS

SOCIAL CHANGE IN THE LAW OF TRUSTS

By

G. W. KEETON, M.A. LL.D.

Professor of English Law and Head of the Department of Laws, University College, London

GREENWOOD PRESS, PUBLISHERS
WESTPORT, CONNECTICUT

Library of Congress Cataloging in Publication Data

Keeton, George Williams, 1902-
Social change in the law of trusts.

Reprint of the 1958 ed. published by Pitman, London.
1. Trusts and trustees--Great Britain. I. Title.
KD1480.K4 1973 346'.42'057 73-9374
ISBN 0-8371-7011-7

First published in 1958 by Sir Isaac Pitman & Sons, Ltd., London

Reprinted with the permission of Professor G. W. Keeton

Reprinted from an original copy in the collections of the University of Illinois Library

Reprinted in 1973 by Greenwood Press, a division of Williamhouse-Regency Inc.

Library of Congress Catalogue Card Number 73-9374

ISBN 0-8371-7011-7

Printed in the United States of America

Preface

This book is in substance a collection of essays which have appeared since 1945 in various legal periodicals, and which were intended to explain some of the problems created in the Law of Trusts by the social changes upon which the country has embarked. Although no attempt is made to present a complete picture it is hoped that these essays do when assembled explain some of the main problems and the attempts which have been made to solve them either by judicial decision or statutory reform. After reflection, it has been decided to leave these essays very much in the form in which they were originally written, although where it seemed necessary references to subsequent changes in the law have been made. I should like to express my thanks to the publishers of *Current Legal Problems*, *The Solicitor* and *The University of Ceylon Law Review* for permission to reproduce the essays which have appeared in those journals.

G. W. Keeton

6 Pump Court,
Temple, E.C.4

15*th August*, 1958

Contents

CHAPTER I

The Selection of Trustees

THE social revolution through which this country has been passing since the end of the recent war has affected every branch of English law in varying degrees. In some branches, the changes are obvious, for they have been brought about by legislation. Thus, the land law has been profoundly affected by the Town and Country Planning Acts, by the Agriculture Act, 1947, and the Agricultural Holdings Act, 1948. In other fields of law, the changes have been less obvious, since they have been brought about by the cumulative effect of judicial decisions, which, in the aggregate, may be almost as far-reaching as legislation. Where this process has taken place, however, or where it is still in progress, its extent may be disguised, because it occurs over a period (in contrast with the immediate impact of legislation), and also because the day-to-day changes which occur as a result of judicial decision are firmly linked with the past, to form a continuous and never-ending process of orderly evolution. The extent of changes of this nature can only be accurately gauged if we survey the product at different points, with a considerable interval of time between them.

One great branch of the law in which almost revolutionary change has occurred, but in which, nevertheless, this change has taken place almost completely unperceived, is the Law of Trusts. The trust, as Maitland long ago pointed out, is a most characteristic product of the English legal genius. It is almost inexplicable without a knowledge of the social environment in which it was developed. For example, it is by no means easy to explain in terms of legal rules, the differences between the medieval use and the modern trust. The task becomes simpler if we remember that the medieval use of land was imposed upon a feoffee for whom feudalism, with its social, economic and political consequences, was still an effective reality, whilst the trust, as it took shape in the eighteenth-century Court of Chancery, was a device by means of which a country landowner in one of the freest societies the world has ever known made provisions of a far-reaching type for the various members of his family. The eighteenth-century decisions which established the modern Law of Trusts are still our leading cases, although the social conditions in which they were decided have now completely passed away. Even in the nineteenth century, settlors and trustees were very different people from their eighteenth-century counterparts. Today, settlors and trustees seem almost to inhabit a different world, in which property is consistently under attack, and in which the thriftiness and foresight of former generations is frequently denounced as anti-social. As might have been predicted, this inversion of social values has produced a harvest of novel and difficult problems within the law of trusts.

The rights and duties of trustees were first settled in detail by the Court of Chancery in the period between the Restoration and the close of the eighteenth century. Many of these were essentially administrative in character, and the standards of care prescribed by the Court of Equity were high. At this period of legal history, there was nothing in any way incongruous in expecting a member of the landowning class to devote considerable time and skill to the gratuitous administration of the property of a neighbour, and to incur heavy legal liability if his judgment proved erroneous. Indeed, at that period the standard of care in the discharge of private responsibilities was probably at its highest. In more recent times, however, the high standards prescribed by the great Equity judges of the eighteenth century have been relaxed by statute. This relaxation reflects changed social conditions. Today, it is becoming increasingly difficult to find persons of ability and standing to undertake the management of private trusts, as the complexity of modern life has steadily increased. For that reason the Trustee Act of 1925, Sect. 23, gave a general power to the trustee to delegate all ordinary routine business of the trust to agents, whom the trustee could remunerate for their services, and for whom (if properly appointed) the trustee was not legally responsible. Thus, it seems probable that in the future a clear division in function will exist between the trustee and his paid agents. The latter will perform ordinary trust business, whilst the activities of the trustee will tend increasingly to be confined to the selection of suitable agents, and to the exercise of the numerous discretions requiring personal judgment, which arise in the execution of a trust. Examples of such discretions (which the trustee may not delegate to an agent) are the determination of the price at which the trustee will sell trust property, or the determination of the proportion of the income of an infant beneficiary's share that the trustee will apply towards the maintenance, education and benefit of an infant beneficiary.

This change, though it has occurred imperceptibly and over a long period, is nevertheless a fundamental one. In the eighteenth century, the trustee-landowner dominated his agents. His general knowledge of affairs was in general superior to theirs, and the occasions when he would have recourse to their advice would usually be few, and they would be for limited purposes only. He would, for example, need a solicitor to conduct the litigation of the trust, but he would usually consider himself better qualified than any employee to decide what investments were proper for the trust, more especially as the range of permissible investments was narrower than it is now. Today, however, our social mechanism has become so complex that the trustee must of necessity rely upon the advice of an increasing number of highly qualified specialist agents, whose advice he ignores at his peril. The Trustee Act, 1925, therefore reflects this change of function when it provides, in Sect. 23 (1) that the trustee is not responsible for such agents if they are appointed in good faith and if they possess the normal professional qualifications. The trustee today is a busy man, who finds it increasingly difficult, because of State interference, to control his own affairs. Increasingly, he has neither the time, nor the capacity, nor the inclination to spend considerable time administering a trust, at any rate where the trust has no direct connection with the affairs of himself or his family. He is therefore progressively becoming the chairman and co-ordinator of a number of professional specialists, who are enabled by statute to charge the usual professional fees for their services, and who incur no more than the customary professional liability for acts done by them in good faith.

This, however, is by no means the full extent of the change. A shortage of trustees of desirable calibre and standing has given rise to the custom of employing corporate trustees. There is the Public Trustee, and there are the trust corporations; and the law of trusts, as it is at present, reflects the transitional period in respect of corporate trusteeship through which we are now passing. The Public Trustee was created by the Public Trustee Act, 1906, to satisfy a long-felt need for an official department which could undertake the administration of trusts of relatively small amount for persons whose range of acquaintances or relatives would not often include many suitable for the office of trustee. Behind such a department there would be the guarantee of the State for proper administration.

In 1956 there was published the Report of a Committee of Inquiry into the working of the Public Trustee Office which indicated that it had scarcely fulfilled the high hopes which were expected at the time of its creation. At that time, with an extremely powerful Liberal Government in office, it was thought that there was need of a statutory corporate trustee who could give a similar, or greater, degree of security to the administration of small and medium-sized estates as was possessed by the larger settlements. Accordingly, the Act itself (Sect. 2 (1)) charges the Public Trustee with the responsibility of administering estates of small value, submitted to him, and he may not decline any estate on account of its smallness (Sect. 2 (3)). Moreover, no question of power to charge for trustee services will arise, for a power to charge is conferred by statute, and in *Re Firth*, Eve, J., thought that there was no valid ground for objection by a beneficiary to the appointment of the Public Trustee because it would involve payment for his services. The existence of the Public Trustee Office has not infrequently proved a boon to trustees or executors who have wished to retire, but who have not found any other persons ready or willing to succeed them. Of course, where the administration involves the carrying on of a business, this method of escape is not open to them, for the Public Trustee may not accept such a trust, or the administration of an insolvent estate, although even in these cases, the Public Trustee may act as custodian trustee, subject to conditions.

Sect. 3 of the Act contains a very useful provision of which, unfortunately, little use has been made. It deals with the case where no one comes forward to administer an estate of small value. Here, if the estate is less than £1,000, any person who would be entitled to apply to the Court for an order of administration, may apply to the Public Trustee to administer it, and when the Public Trustee accepts in writing, the trust property vests in him.

The Act also provided that the Public Trustee Office should from time to time set up branch offices. Indeed, had the work warranted it, something like a national service in numerous large towns might have come into existence. Only one branch was established, however, in Manchester, and the recent committee of inquiry have now recommended that this should be closed for lack of work. Meanwhile, even in London, although the work has grown steadily, progress has been slow, and the proportion of work done by the Public Trustee Office in relation to that done by other trust corporations, and by private trustees, has steadily declined. Thus, in 1913, the Public Trustee's share of grants of probate to trust corporations was 200 out of 290. By 1933, the share was 500 out of 2,380. As the committee notes, in the first years after 1908, when the Public Trustee Office was established, it had virtually a monopoly of corporate trustee work. When, in 1920, the Court was empowered to grant probate to a trust corporation by its corporate name, and when this was followed by the Trustee Act of 1925, which facilitated administration by corporate trustees, the executor and trustee departments of banks and insurance companies entered increasingly into the field. Even so, however, they were, and still are, handicapped, as compared with the Public Trustee, for except when they act as custodian trustees under the

Public Trustee Rules, they have no statutory power to charge, and accordingly, some trusts have to be rejected by them for lack of a charging clause, although the exact figures are unknown. Before the war, an effort was made to get round this limitation by providing, on the retirement of individual trustees in favour of trust corporations, that the trust corporation should be appointed (*a*) as custodian trustee, and (*b*) as managing trustee. In *Forster* v. *Deacons Bank Ltd.*, and again in *Arning* v. *James*, it was held that these attempts were destitute of legal effect, and therefore the disability of trust corporations remains, although it will doubtless be removed when a new Trustee Act is drafted. In the meanwhile, however, in spite of this handicap the trust corporations have far outstripped the Public Trustee in two important respects: (1) the volume of trustee work they do; and (2) the size of the estates they administer, for analysis shows that they administer far more small estates than the Public Trustee does.

The reasons are not far to seek, and they reflect no discredit on the Public Trustee. If a man has need of an insurance company, and still more if a life insurance policy is linked up with house purchase, it is not unnatural that he should be content to have his affairs handled by the insurance company after his death. It is an equally understandable reaction that a man should be willing to permit the bank which has handled his account during his life to wind up his estate on death, especially if, as is often the case, his securities and documents of title lie in the bank's strong-room. The Public Trustee Office, by contrast, undertakes little publicity[1] and has no other point of contact with the general public. The result has been that the Public Trustee Office has, in the past, been used mainly by testators of the comfortable and upper middle classes. As these progressively decline, there is very real danger that the work of the Public Trustee Office will also decline. At any rate, it has worked at a loss, and over the years, there has been a deficit on trustee work of no less than £187,145. Although, in present budgetary terms, this sum is negligible, it hints at waning interest and acceptance of this is implicit in the Committee's report, and in the Government's

[1] This is now increasing.

action on it. The Government have rejected a recommendation that an Exchequer grant should be made to cover the loss in administering estates of small value. Instead, increased efforts will be made to achieve economies in running the Public Trustee Office. Thus, the property advisers section is to be wound up, and the Office will in future obtain professional advice in the usual way. Moreover, surplus accommodation at the London office is to be let at an economic rent.

These are all steps in the right direction, but they inevitably raise a further question. Is a Public Trustee Office today necessary at all? When it was established half a century ago, the modern trust corporation was in its infancy, and was subject to all kinds of handicaps in administration. Some of these handicaps have now gone, but it is time the remainder disappeared. Moreover, the danger of finding no one to administer small estates, so present in the minds of the legislators of 1906, has proved largely illusory, and in any case, the existence of the Public Trustee Office has not solved the question of administering such estates. It may be suggested that the time has now come for considering whether trust corporations should be given a statutory power to charge, and the Public Trustee Office abolished. As a state service, in this country at any rate, the case for a state trustee hardly seems to have been proved. Even if the Public Trustee Office remains, but this out-of-date restriction is removed, more and more trust work will pass to trust corporations. Indeed, in the future, solicitors and trust corporations may possibly enjoy almost a monopoly in this field. Each of these two types of trustee has its advantages. The solicitor often has the advantage of personal knowledge of settlor and beneficiaries, and his legal knowledge is of the first importance. On the other hand, the trust corporation has the advantage of absolute security, and it offers the service of the experts it employs. This, however, is not an unqualified blessing, for the expert staff of a trust corporation may see technical difficulties which are of small account in practice, with possible applications to court in doubtful cases becoming somewhat numerous.

One further point of distinction between the private trustee and the paid corporate trustee is slowly emerging: the law will exact a higher standard of care from the trust corporation, to the extent that it will rarely, if ever, be able to claim the benefit of Sect. 61 of the Trustee Act, 1925.

The growth in the practice of employing corporate trustees, as we have seen, is the consequence of changed social conditions, resulting in the absence of suitable persons to fill the office of private trustee. Is it possible to probe a little deeper into the extent and implications of this great change? I think that it is. The typical trustee of the eighteenth century, it has been suggested, was the country landowner, who managed his estate thriftily, stood high in the estimation of the county, and almost certainly took his place upon the Bench at Quarter Sessions. Indeed, if we think of Addison's Sir Roger de Coverley we shall not be far wrong. By the second half of the nineteenth century he has changed greatly. He has become a professional man or a member of some well-established firm. He may sit upon one or two boards of directors, but if he does it will only be after a careful scrutiny of the company's business, and it will be with the intention of exercising vigilance in supervising the conduct of the company's business. Though he may be generous in his private affairs, he will be careful even to the point of parsimony in the expenditure of public money, and he will possess to a marked degree that nice and unheated judgment which, in the nineteenth century, was such a striking characteristic of the English upper middle class business man, with a public school background. In fact, if one wishes to see a full-length portrait of the ideal trustee of this period it is to be found in the pages the *Forsyte Saga*, in Galsworthy's *Man of Property*, Soames Forstye.

If we were to inquire today, however, why trustees of the calibre of nineteenth-century middle class business men or their eighteenth-century predecessors are no longer forthcoming, it would be necessary to write a long and depressing chapter of social history. Both of them lived well by modern standards. They worked hard, and they preserved (and sometimes enlarged) the produce of their labours with great skill. Yet they drew heavily upon their leisure in furtherance of those innumerable public services without which the mechanism of public life cannot run smoothly. They sat in Parliament, they served on benches of magistrates, they were churchwardens, hospital governors and trustees. They had, in fact, a genius for committees, and it was in consequence of their outlook, that the committee system became the automatic means of transacting public business in England. Moreover, all these public services were performed, not only without payment of salary, but without payment of expenses. It is only in our own time that the "service principle" has been erected into a dogma, and that simultaneously we have made generous payments for "expenses" and broken time in respect of the performance of a public duty.

Two world wars, and a social revolution during the last half-century have gone far towards destroying this class. Increasingly large sections of industrial and commercial activity are being placed outside the range of private enterprise altogether. Again, present rates of taxation make it impossible for a professional or business man to contemplate retirement at approximately sixty years of age, with the prospect of ten or fifteen years of public service before him. He must remain in harness almost to the day of his death, and since the conduct of his business has become incomparably more exacting than it was half a century ago, he has neither time nor energy to devote to public or quasi-public activities. Moreover, more unhappily, since the conclusion of the second world war there has gradually developed an attitude of mind that the services of the property-owning classes are somewhat tainted. Not unnaturally, therefore, they have become a little reluctant to tender services which have so obviously not been wanted.

It may perhaps be suggested, however, that if the problem of the vanishing trustee is at bottom a social one, in due course a new race of trustees will arise from a different social background. Of that, however, there is as yet no sign at all. The whole trend of development in the law of trusts has hitherto favoured the middle class trustee. It is not that the trustee requires expert knowledge. Indeed, today, as we have seen, that is no longer true, for he is able to employ and pay whatever expert agents he may deem to be necessary for the discharge of trust duties. Nevertheless, the trustee must be, as in the past he must always have been, a man of affairs. He must have familiarity with the responsibilities of managing real property. He must know the implications of entering into a mortgage. He must keep some kind of watch upon the financial position of the country, so that he can decide what changes should be made in the condition of trustee investments. He must know, in general terms, at least, the effect of the modern avalanche of legislation upon the property which is subject to the trust. These, and innumerable similar decisions arising in the administration of a trust, can only rarely be suitably made by those who live in council houses, who earn a weekly wage, and do not operate a banking account. If present tendencies continue unchecked, it is possible to foresee the time when the law of trusts will be as obsolete as the law relating to widow's dower. In the transitional period, however, we shall employ increasingly the paid corporate trustee.

CHAPTER II

Trustee Investments

So far only the personal qualities of the trustee, and the increasing difficulty of finding suitable persons to fill the office have been considered. It is time now to turn to his functions. The primary and over-riding duty of the trustee is to get in, preserve and administer the trust fund. This may come into the hands of the trustee either in a properly invested state (as will frequently occur where a trust is created during the settlor's lifetime, or as a fund which it is necessary to put into a proper state of investment. Even in the first case, problems of reinvestment will frequently arise.

The root concept of trust property is just as much conditioned by its social background as the conception of the trustee is. The underlying assumption is that wealth can be accumulated in sufficient quantity within a reasonable time, so that when invested the income arising from it will be adequate for a number of social purposes, whether it be the maintenance of successive members of a family or the support of some charitable purpose, such as a church or a college. If national policy is aimed, as since the war it has been deliberately aimed, to frustrate those two purposes, then sooner or later they will fail. Already, far-reaching changes in our national habits have taken place. Today, it is no longer certain sections of the lower classes which live simply from week to week. It is virtually the entire community. In a period of inflation and currency devaluation there is indeed little possibility of an alternative. This, however, has as its inescapable consequence the fact that the natural desire of a man of ability to provide for his immediate descendants, and the desire of public-spirited persons to provide for the continuance of voluntary activities to which they attach importance can no longer be satisfied. In both cases the country is the poorer, in more than one sense.

However, altogether apart from this ominous symptom, the trustee today is faced with other problems which add very greatly to his difficulties. Today, society has become so complex that he must rely on expert advice, where his predecessor in the eighteenth and nineteenth centuries would have trusted in his own judgment. If the trustee wishes to turn a field into a recreation ground, or if he wishes to turn a substantial old house into flats, he will have to seek planning permission. He will have to enter into prolonged negotiations with a multitude of officials and public bodies through the intermediary of solicitor and architect. Even when he has incurred all this preliminary expenditure he may find his application refused or, even if it is granted, he may find that he is unable to procure materials, or labour, or both, to achieve what he wants. Thus, altogether apart from the question of taxation, which is heavily penal in amount, the trustee is faced with the certainty that the income and capital of the fund will be increasingly employed upon purposes which, though necessary having regard to the strange times in which we live, have no direct relation to the purpose for which his trust was constituted. In other words, administrative costs have risen many times in amount, whilst income yields have declined sharply. Just before the second world war there was a severe famine in Shensi, one of the remotest provinces of north-west China. The United States, with characteristic generosity, dispatched cargoes of wheat to Shanghai for the relief of famine. When it was put ashore it was placed on the railway and addressed to Shensi. Unfortunately, however, China had customs posts at provincial frontiers, and at each of these a portion of the wheat was sold to meet customs dues. The rest was found insufficient to pay the rail charges, and was therefore sold *en route*. In consequence the famine continued without American relief. The law of trusts is today approaching a comparable state. Administration costs increasingly swallow up declining revenues.

It has been pointed out that income yields from trust funds are steadily declining. The main reasons for this are the high rate of taxation and the ever-increasing cost of administration. Another factor of almost equal importance is inflation. The full history of trustee investments has never been written. It is a chapter in the history of Great Britain's rise to the position of the world's banker, and of her rapid fall from that position in the past two decades. When the law of trusts was re-created by Lord Nottingham and his successors at the end of the seventeenth century, there existed no settled practice with regard to trustee investments. In the carefree days of Charles II a government loan would have emphatically not been a good trustee investment, and the position of trustees at this point was one of great uncertainty. Wise and honest trustees sought the advice of the Court. Others were less scrupulous, and employed trust funds in the furtherance of their own interests. This had disastrous consequences at the beginning of the eighteenth century, with the bursting of the South Sea Bubble, for we are told that one of the circumstances which aggravated the general ruin was that many trustees had yielded to the nation-wide gambling fever, and had speculated in South Sea and similar stock with funds committed to their care. The full story of the ensuing misery has never been told, but there can be no doubt that its effect upon the practice of the Court of Chancery was salutary, for the Court began to draw a sharp line between investments which it was proper for the trustee to make, and those which were not. Moreover, the Chancellors laid down the great equitable principle that a trustee may not profit from his trust, thereby removing the incentive of personal gain from the trustee's power to make investments. There can be little doubt that the chastening experience of the South Sea Bubble had a good deal to do with the stricter formulation of this rule. Thus Lord Macclesfield held in *Bromfield* v. *Wytherly*, as late as 1719, that "if an executor or trustee of money places it out in the funds, or on other security, whereby he gains considerably, he shall have the whole benefit thereof to himself, in respect of the hazard he ran of being a considerable loser thereby, which he must have borne." It is only when the trustee is actually insolvent (!) when he invests that he may not keep the profit, since he would have been unable to satisfy the loss. This decision was on the eve of the wild orgy of speculation which drove the price of £100 worth of South Sea Stock from £130 on January 31, 1720, to £1,000 in May, and to £1,060 at mid-summer of the same year. Lord Macclesfield had certainly made it easy for trustees to enrich themselves at the expense of their beneficiaries. Seven years later, however, with the full effects of the financial disaster now apparent, Lord King sternly laid down in *Keech* v. *Sandford* the principle that a trustee may never profit personally from his trust, adding: "I very well see, if a trustee, on refusal to renew, might have a lease for himself, few trust estates would be renewed to *cestuis que use.*" This was not cynicism. It was recent bitter experience.

Decisions such as this had the effect of discouraging trustees from hazarding their beneficiaries' property, whether for their own enrichment, or for any other reason. It was only gradually, however, that the complementary rule that trustees *must* put trust money in proper investments developed. In between, there was an awkward transitional period, during which trustees were not compelled to invest at all, and they often let trust money lie idle for fear of loss. Since, however, such a practice went some way towards frustrating the very purpose for which trusts were normally created, *i.e.* the enjoyment of a number of interests in succession, it became common to incorporate into trust instruments clauses giving trustees express powers to lend out money at interest. As the eighteenth century progressed, and successive Chancellors of the Exchequer placed British finances and Government loans on an entirely new basis, Government stock at three per cent became an investment which was very much sought after. Moreover, since the Court of Chancery invested funds under its control in these stocks (which, when consolidated later in the century, became known as Consols) the rule developed that a trustee was free to invest in them, without personal liability, even without authorisation from the settlor. So began that increasingly important alliance between Government and investing middle classes, for the national benefit;

an alliance which has been terminated only in our own day, as the consequence of the triumph of another conception of social organisation, *i.e.* the so-called planned welfare State.

During the eighteenth century, however, each progressive extension of the national debt simply became an aspect of increased national wealth; and although there were Jeremiahs who darkly predicted that such an expansion of credit could not go on, British overseas trade expanded so rapidly that there was constantly an abundance of investible money seeking Government stocks, which therefore remained remarkably steady, even in temporary periods of national difficulty.

In the nineteenth century there were further developments. Following the reform of English local government, by the Municipal Corporations Act, 1835, trustees were progressively encouraged to invest in the loans of municipal corporations, and later still, in those of the new county authorities. In the second half of the nineteenth century, the area of investment was extended to include the stocks of dominion and colonial governments, as well as those of the growing municipalities of the Empire. Trust money, therefore, played a part of first importance, not only in financing the wars with France in the eighteenth century, with the resulting expansion of Empire and enormous growth of commerce, but in the development of the resources of that empire, and with it the growth of self-government in the nineteenth century. The nineteenth century, however, posed one other problem of major importance for the trustee. The rapid growth of industry, made possible by the invention of the steam engine and the growth of railways, raised the question of the extent to which trustees could properly participate in these enterprises. Towards the middle of the nineteenth century there was a fever of speculation in railways which in some ways recalled the madness of the years of the South Sea Bubble. On both occasions there were enterprises which, if they had been permitted to develop normally, would have been of great service to the community. When they became pawns in a nationwide stock-jobbing boom, however, they proved unable to support the extravagant hopes which had been raised, and some of them failed. Even the surviving railways suffered from over-lavish capitalisation. This time, however, trustees were more rigidly limited in their capacity to make investments than they had been at the beginning of the eighteenth century. Statute prescribed that they could only invest in the debentures or preference shares of railways which had paid a dividend of four per cent on their ordinary shares during the preceding ten years. As far as industrial undertakings were concerned, participation by the trustee was excluded altogether, unless the settlor expressly authorised it. This probably represented the best attainable compromise between security of capital and large income yield that could be achieved. After all, the leading nineteenth-century cases governing the mode of apportionment of assets between capital and income regarded four per cent as a reasonable average income from trustee investments regarded collectively. This, in an age when income tax dropped to twopence in the pound and when indirect taxation was of almost negligible proportions, was no bad yield. There were not many trustees who agreed with Timothy Forsyte that the only prudent policy was to avoid even investments permitted by successive Trustee Acts, and to limit their range to the sacred inviolability of three per cent Consols, which rose higher and higher in popular estimation as the reign of Victoria lengthened.

It used to be a commonplace among the elderly to say that things have never been the same "since the old Queen died," and from the point of view of the trustee, this is certainly true. Wars and rumours of wars cause even "gilt-edged securities" to fluctuate in price, but even worse has ensued. Since 1914 one of the trustee's very real embarrassments has been the impossibility of planning ahead. Income tax and allied taxes have varied constantly, usually for the worse, and death duties have progressively confiscated more and more of the fund which the trustee administered. To add to his difficulties there has been greater interference with interest yields between 1914 and 1957 than there was in the entire period from 1700 to 1914. It is true that in the second half of the nineteenth century one Chancellor of the Exchequer, Goschen, sought to take advantage of the prevailing prosperity and an abundance of money to force down the rate of interest on Government stocks from three per cent to two and a half per cent, but his efforts were not well received, and they proved a failure, since the capital value of the stocks quickly slumped to the point where the real yield was again three per cent. The national effort in the first world war involved expenditure on a quite unprecedented scale, and the need for new capital was so great that the rate of interest on War Loans rose rapidly to five per cent, where it remained until the great conversion loan of 1931 reduced the rate to three and a half per cent where, substantially, it remained throughout the second world war. After 1945, however, there was apparently lighthearted experimentation with the lower yield of two and a half per cent. Unfortunately, the "Dalton 2½s," as they are often called, after a short interval fell to such a point that the effective yield again became substantially the same as that of other stocks. Similar consequences have followed over-lavish issue of Government stock at low interest rates by way of compensation for property taken under successive Nationalisation Acts. Where these results have followed in respect of trust property, the trustee has once again been compelled to stand by whilst the capital of the trust fund is arbitrarily reduced by Government action. Thus, in 1957 the market price of long-dated 2½s fell to 50 and even lower,[1] so that over half the capital had been lost by those who had been rash enough (or unfortunate enough) to take them up on issue.

Today, therefore the task of keeping up the fund of a private trust is one of unprecedented complexity. Indeed, it has become almost an impossible task, and in face of growing difficulties settlors have been compelled to give trustees wider powers than have been general hitherto. They are permitting them to invest in securities of any kind, provided the trustees exercise their powers in good faith, and the courts, after initial hesitation, have now accepted the implications of this wider power to the extent that they have refrained from holding trustees liable if they act in good faith and loss ensues.

[1] 44½ in September 1957, following the raising of the Bank Rate to 7 per cent.

Thus, there is today no doubt that a trustee has power to invest in commercial stocks and shares or in land under a clause which states that "all moneys requiring to be invested under this my will may be invested by the trustee in any manner in which he may in his absolute discretion think fit in all respects as if he were the sole beneficial owner of such moneys."[1] This is, indeed, inevitable, for if the trust extends to shares in public utilities or heavy industry, trustees will have the choice of standing by whilst the fund is reduced by the unsatisfactory terms of exchange for Government stock which appear in the Nationalisation Acts, or of selling under depreciatory conditions and then investing the proceeds in Government stock, with low income yields, and the capital value of which fluctuates dangerously in successive national crises. Even if the fund is simply invested in long-term Government stocks (as Timothy Forsyte would have wished), unless the fund is an extremely large one, the result is that no one is able to live upon the excessively diminished yields. It may perhaps be suggested that under modern political and social theories nobody should expect to live upon the produce of capital; yet even today many of the clauses of family settlements are concerned with the elderly, the widowed, the infirm, and with children. Moreover, there are other factors which must be weighed. Some years ago Parliament considered a bill introduced for the purpose of varying the terms under which Lady Mountbatten enjoyed the property bequeathed under the terms of her grandfather's will. The Cassel estate was an unusually large one, and Lady Mountbatten enjoyed an extremely large interest in it. Unfortunately for her, however, she inherited it subject to a restraint on anticipation, which meant that she could not alienate the capital or future income. She could simply spend the current income as it fell due. Although restraints on anticipation were abolished for future settlements in 1935, this Act did not affect restraints imposed in an instrument which was already in operation, and accordingly Lady Mountbatten's estate was unaffected by it. Nevertheless, although the capital value of Lady Mountbatten's estate is to be computed in millions, it

[1] *Re Power's Will Trusts; Re Harari's Settlement Trusts.*

was stated in the House of Commons that taxation had reduced her income from £80,000 to £4,500 a year. The object of the Mountbatten Bill was therefore to enable Lady Mountbatten to set aside the restraint on anticipation so as to use the capital of her trust fund. Eventually, however, this private bill was withdrawn, and there was introduced the Married Women (Restraint upon Anticipation) Bill[1]—a public bill having as its object the abolition of surviving restraints on anticipation. The bill was based on two main principles—the undesirability of preserving any remaining mark of the married woman's former subordinate status, and the hardship arising from inability to touch capital when income yields are inadequate to support the beneficiary. If the position of Lady Mountbatten, as the principal beneficiary under one of the largest trusts of modern times, was what it was stated to be in the House of Commons on the second reading of this bill, what is the position with regard to family trusts of persons of ordinary means?

When the problem is seen in these terms it will be apparent that the law of trusts is today grappling with a problem which goes to the roots of our social existence. In the past the prosperity of these islands has depended to a substantial degree upon the prudence and foresight of successive generations of investors, of whom trustees, whether private or charitable, were an important—perhaps the most important—element. The prosperity arising from their investments was two-fold. On the one hand it ensured the availability of an adequate supply of capital for the development of public services in this country, the Dominions and Colonies. Moreover, the long-term investment which is possible, and even desirable, for trustees, was an important steadying factor in times of war or national crisis. On the other hand, the possibility of secure investment, with fixed and low income yields was an instrument for giving the steadily-expanding middle class a stake in the country, and for providing the means whereby that class provided for the education and maintenance of its children, and for the support and comfort of its older members. These habits were of long standing, and in so far as they

[1] Now the Married Women (Restraint of Anticipation) Act, 1949.

were induced by the machinery of the law of trusts, they date from the Revolution of 1688 at the latest. Today, however, the edifice which has been laboriously built up is in danger of collapsing. There is no longer any certainty that the desired ends can be achieved, nor can the trust be preserved for a prolonged period. The alliance between the State's welfare and the thrift of its most industrious members has been impaired to such a degree that there is real danger that it may not survive at all; and it is no accident that, as these ominous changes have taken place, national economic difficulties have increased. It may be, of course, that present policies will be pursued to the point where private property itself ceases to exist as a considerable factor in social organisation. If, on the other hand, national recovery is to be sought along less drastic lines, then the desirability of maintaining the trust as a social institution, and of simplifying the task of the trustee in the course of his administration is evident.

Two other limitations on the trustee's power of investment require brief notice. The trustee possesses a statutory power to invest in the mortgage of freehold property up to two-thirds of the ascertained value of the property. There is no similar power to invest in the mortgage of personal property. Accordingly, if a trustee lends money on the security of an insurance policy, or of share certificates, it is always at his risk, unless the trust deed expressly exempts him. Secondly, in spite of the inclusion in the Trustee Act, 1925, of a clause (Sect. 10 (3)), difficulties have been experienced both before and since 1926 where a trustee was authorised by a trust instrument (possibly a will) to retain shares in a commercial enterprise (possibly a family business) and a merger with some other business was desired.

Before 1926 the decisions of the courts erred possibly on the side of over-caution. They held that in such a situation, the trustee had no powers to concur in an amalgamation, or reconstruction, since the result would be that he would hold shares of a type different from those authorised by the trust deed. They also went further, and held that the Court itself could not authorise the trustee to enter into such transactions, except in accordance with "salvage principles." This meant that the Court would authorise the trustee to concur in a reconstruction or amalgamation where failure to do so would be to cause the shares to become a total loss, but not where the result of the transaction was expected to be the earning of a larger profit. Thus the Court only allowed the trustee to join in the amalgamation where his property was already approaching the danger area, even if it had not actually entered it. The result was that unless other shareholders were prepared to buy out the trustee, the merger or amalgamation could not proceed.[1]

The difficulties involved in this situation were so apparent that the Trustee Act, 1925, sought to remedy them. By Sect. 10 (3) of that Act, trustees were given a general power to concur in the amalgamation or reconstruction of companies in which they held shares. This effort to remove cramping limitations has unhappily largely failed to achieve its purpose, for the Court held in 1935 that the section did not cover an exchange of shares with a holding company. Moreover, the decision went further. The Trustee Act, 1925, in Sect. 57, had given the Court power in general terms to sanction transactions for the benefit of the trust, for which the trustees possessed no specific power, but the Court held that this did not cover an exchange of shares with a holding company.[2]

It is not only in England that trustee investments have proved a recurring problem. The laws of the forty-nine states of the American Union, as one would expect, show wide diversities in viewpoint on the proper field of investment for trustees. At one end of the scale, the constitutions of the states of Alabama, Wyoming, Montana and Colorado provide that no act of the state legislature may authorise the investment of funds by trustees in commercial enterprises. At the other end of the scale the law of Arizona permits trustees to invest funds "in the best manner in their powers, or as the Court may direct," and the law of the state of California confers a similar freedom in rather different terms.

An important and growing group of states follows what is termed the Massachusetts or "prudent man" rule. This rule,

[1] *Re New; Re Tollemache.* [2] *Re Walker's Settlement.*

originating in Massachusetts, provides that a trustee "must observe how men of prudence, discretion, and intelligence manage their own affairs, not in regard to speculation, but in regard to the permanent disposition of their funds, considering the probable income, as well as the probable safety of the capital to be invested."

Connecticut, Rhode Island, Maine, Maryland, Vermont and Michigan are among the states which follow this rule. Until recent times New York followed a different practice which took its name from that state, and which is still followed in a substantially larger number of states than the Massachusetts rule. This practice is the American counterpart to existing British practice. On the whole, the less developed states have imposed the heaviest restrictions on investment whilst the older and more commercial states have allowed wider discretion, and investment in the shares of commercial and industrial enterprises.

From this point of view the position of New York was a little anomalous, but an important, and possibly decisive, change in American practice occurred in 1950. On 1st July of that year an Act of New York State completely changed trustee investment policy by enacting the "prudent man" rule. Partly because so much trust business is transacted in the state of New York, and partly because the New York rule has governed the practice of the largest group of states in the American Union, it has been widely thought in America that this important change presages the eventual adoption of the "prudent man" rule by all the states of the Union.

Having regard to American developments, the Report of the Nathan Committee on Charitable Trusts, published in 1953[1] is extremely interesting. The Report recommends that all trustees (not merely those of charitable trusts) should be permitted to invest up to 50 per cent of the funds under their control in the debentures and stock and shares (including equity stock and shares) of financial, industrial and commercial companies quoted on the stock exchange. Three extremely important paragraphs of the Report summarise

[1] Cmd. 8710.

the effect of social unheavals of the last half-century. They read as follows—

> 285. The principal changes in this respect are—
>
> (*a*) the recurrence of major wars, resulting in a vast destruction of wealth, the uneconomic use of labour and materials, and the overthrow of governments and national states;
>
> (*b*) the abandonment of the gold standard and the exchange convertibility based thereon;
>
> (*c*) the larger degree of intervention by governments in economic life, including the exercise of the financial powers formerly exercised by the central banks.
>
> 286. If a long view is taken, inflation appears to be a natural tendency of currencies and the trend of the last fifty years may be regarded as merely an acceleration of this natural tendency. The acceleration has, however, become a matter of grave anxiety; the real value even of the soundest currency has been greatly reduced.
>
> 287. There is no indication that the inflationary tendency of currencies is likely to be reversed and this forms the major problem of the trustee, whose range of investment is confined to fixed interest money stocks. The restrictions, intended as a safeguard, have become a source of danger.

Commenting on the proposals of the Nathan Report, a writer in *The Times* of 16th January, 1953, suggested that, as an alternative to the adoption in England of the "prudent man" rule, either entirely, or in respect of one half of the trust funds, the trustee might be permitted to invest in the shares of recognised investment trust companies, and also that the price at which such an investment trust is prepared to buy shares should be the basis of the value for extra duty purposes. The writer further suggested that this range of investment should be open also to pension funds, including the National Insurance Fund. These observations represent what is today essentially a conservative view.

On the other hand, a leading article in *The Financial Times* of 17th December, 1952, thought that such a limited extension would serve little practical purpose. It urged that the object should be, as the Nathan Report suggests, to take in whole classes of stocks, including debentures and preference stocks (with adequate safeguards concerning their priorities).

The article added that there would naturally be diversity of view concerning the inclusion of equities, but here again safeguards could be devised to minimise the effects of imprudence.

It is not only that the conditions of investment today bear no resemblance to those prevailing a century ago. In addition, the growth of great industrial and commercial undertakings, with a carefully regulated capital structure, gives opportunities for reasonably safe investment which did not exist a century ago, and offer possibilities of capital gain in place of the depreciation which in recent years has continuously affected gilt-edged securities. All these factors are felt increasingly by beneficiaries under private trusts, whose incomes have been startlingly diminished by penal taxation, and whose funds will suffer similar mutilation where there is a succession on death.

There is, however, another aspect of the situation which is of the widest national importance. Funds available for fresh industrial development have shrunk to small proportions, also as a result of excessive taxation. If fresh sources of investment are to be made available, recourse must be had to trust funds. It is in this respect that the recommendations of the Nathan Report are not only in harmony with recent trends in the United States, but they also show an awareness of our own domestic needs at the present time. Too much, however, should not be expected to result from such a change of policy as is advocated by the Report. Many trustees would no doubt continue to play for safety by investing in "gilt-edged," even with capital depreciation, so long as their favoured position in law remains. Those who ventured outside the range of gilt-edged would no doubt tread cautiously for some time to come. Nevertheless, the Report does offer a way out from restrictions which are now generally felt to be irksome, and from which small trust funds, without special investment clauses, are the greatest losers. It is therefore very greatly to be regretted that no legislation embodying these recommendations of the Nathan Committee has so far been drafted.

CHAPTER III

The Duke of Norfolk's Case and the Perpetuity Rule

1. The Duke of Norfolk's Case

THREE recent publications have directed attention afresh to the importance of the *Duke of Norfolk's* case in relation to the Rule Against Perpetuities. They are the Report of the Law Reform Committee on the Rule Against Perpetuities,[1] a few months after the appearance of the full survey of the rule in the monograph on *The Rule Against Perpetuities* by Dr. J. H. C. Morris and Professor Barton Leach. This survey extends to the development of the rule on both sides of the Atlantic, for it was taken to the United States by the early settlers. In some states, the Rule was abolished by legislation in favour of some simple test of remoteness, only to be restored again by a later statute. As the authors observe: "state after state has repealed its statute and re-established the common law rule. It is believed that this is a sequence of events unique in the history of the common law. It is extraordinary that a rule having its origin nearly three centuries ago has proved more workable than modern attempts to provide substitutes for it".[2]

Finally, in the seventy-third volume of the Selden Society's publications which, with Volume 74, is devoted to Lord Nottingham's Cases,[3] fresh light is thrown upon the original decision itself. In the Introduction to that volume, the editor surveys the gradual development of the Perpetuity Rule prior to 1682, and explains the reasons which led Lord Nottingham to defend the rule in terms which have governed the law of property, and especially the law of settlements ever since. Both

[1] (1956) Cmnd. 18.

[2] P. 13.

[3] *Lord Nottingham's Cases*. Edited by Dr. E. C. Yale.

Gray[1] and Holdsworth[2] had already traced the history of the Rule somewhat fully, and the work of Dr. Yale therefore serves as a most valuable commentary upon it.

The decision is, in perspective, a step, and a most important one, in the policy of the judiciary to preserve the alienability of land. Already in *Taltarum's* case in 1472, the courts had given their sanction to the devices of fines and recoveries as a method of defeating the unbarrable entail which owed its origin to the statute *De donis conditionalibus*, 1285. Once again the landowners attempted to evade the effects of *Taltarum's* case by inserting a "clause of perpetuity" into their settlements. This clause provided that whenever a tenant in tail should attempt to bar the entail, the land should pass as if he were dead, or as if he were dead without issue. Such clauses, however, were held void in a group of cases at the beginning of the seventeenth century[3] and these ended the attempts to create unbarrable entails directly under the statute.

An alternative line of approach was by way of contingent remainders, but these were so liable to destruction that they were of little value in the attempt to preserve alienability, until the device of trustees to preserve contingent remainders was introduced. This is, of course, a device which will always be associated with the name of Sir Orlando Bridgman, and it was said to be due to a desire to increase the efficacy of settlements during the Civil Wars, but Pollock points out that limitations somewhat similar in form were already in use at an earlier period.[4] The validity of this device seems to have been first accepted by the courts in 1697.[5] Yet another problem arose with the Statute of Uses, 1535, and the Statute of Wills, 1540. These statutes turned future interests, formerly equitable under a use, into legal estates. If such executory limitations were indestructible, then a new method of creating "perpetuities" had come into existence. Once again, however, the courts intervened, and held that if a limitation could take effect as a contingent remainder, it must be so construed; and so it became liable to destruction.[6]

[1] *Perpetuities:* see ss. 123–200. [2] *History of English Law*, Vol. VII.
[3] *Corbet's Case; Mildmay's Case; Mary Portington's Case.*
[4] *The Land Laws*, p. 224. [5] *Duncomb* v. *Duncomb.*
[6] *Chudleigh's Case; Purefoy* v. *Rogers.*

Another attempt to produce a perpetuity was made by the creation of successive life estates to a person and his issue. This was attacked by Coke in *Perrot's* case, where he lays down the principle which was always thereafter accepted, that the estate may be limited to the unborn son of a living person, but further limitations, to the unborn son of that unborn son, and to remoter issue, are void. This rule, usually known as the Rule in *Whitby* v. *Mitchell* survived until 1925, when the Law of Property Act, 1925, abolished it for instruments coming into operation after 1925. This rule is sometimes known as the old rule against perpetuities, though its antiquity was always rather doubtful.[1] It was, in any event, unnecessary, once the modern rule had been developed.

Still a further attempt towards perpetuity was made by means of executory devises of terms of years. In two important cases at the beginning of the seventeenth century[2] it was held that executory devises in a term of years after a life interest, were not only good but indestructible. These decisions are attributed by Lord Nottingham in the *Duke of Norfolk's* case to the influence of the Court of Chancery, and a few years later the common law courts decided in *Pells* v. *Brown* to escape from the cramping effects of earlier decisions, and to hold that an executory devise of freehold land, which could not take effect as a contingent remainder, was indestructible. Dr. Yale suggests that this decision may also have been due to Chancery pressure.

The next stage in the history of these early attempts to define perpetuity is traced in detail by Dr. Yale. Gray, and following him, all the later writers, have stressed the restrictive effect of the decision of the Court of Exchequer Chamber in *Child* v. *Baylie*. In that case a term was devised to A and his assigns, provided that if A died without issue living at his death, then the term was to go over to B. Although the gift over to B was no more remote than that in *Manning's* case it was held bad. Various reasons were advanced but one most readily perceivable at this distance of time is the illogical one that in *Manning's* case the limitation had followed a life interest,

[1] See Morris and Barton Leach, pp. 250–3.

[2] *Manning's* case; *Lampet's* case.

and in *Child* v. *Baylie* it followed an estate tail. Plucknett, however, sees in the argument of Davenport in this case the first hint of attention being paid to the importance of the life in being.[1] Yale, on the other hand prefers to postpone this change on emphasis until 1662. In the decision of Lord Chancellor Clarendon, with Foster and Bridgman, C.JJ. and Hale, C.B., in *Goring* v. *Bickerstaff* there was a limitation to a succession of living persons in remainder, following a life estate, and it was held that this could not be a perpetuity, "otherwise, if the persons were not in being."

Some effort to establish a clear principle was obviously needed, if conveyancing practice was to be firmly established and if settlements were to be placed on a firm foundation. Yale, however, shows in his Introduction that Lord Nottingham's formulation of the Rule in the *Duke of Norfolk's* case was the product of cautious experiment, and not of sudden inspiration. In *Burges* v. *Burges* a lease was limited in trust for a husband for life, afterwards to his wife for life, then to their first and other sons successively and the heirs of their bodies, remainder to the daughters, remainder to the husband and wife and their heirs. The husband was twice married, a daughter being the only child of the first marriage, whilst there were two sons and a daughter of the second marriage. Lord Nottingham decreed the lease to the second wife as administratrix to the husband and all the remainders void, though there was a daughter by the first marriage and the contingent remainders to the sons in tail never happened. Twice more in the year 1674, in *Oakes* v. *Chalfont*, and again in *Knight* v. *Knight*, he is seen to be grappling with the same problem. Finally, in the *Duke of Norfolk's* case, Lord Nottingham was prepared to set out his considered views as a coherent doctrine. In doing so, he reviewed the entire history of the struggle against perpetuities, stating the points established by the earlier cases, and adding that the rules bound the Chancery as much as they did the common law courts. It is important to appreciate, as Dr. Yale points out, that his decision was based on reasons of law, and not on principles of natural equity or conscience.

[1] *Concise History of the Common Law*, 5th Ed., p. 597.

The decision of Lord Nottingham was not without its critics, for the heads of the common law courts, whom he had consulted, had all thought the settlement bad, and one of them, North, C.J.C.P., who succeeded Lord Nottingham as Lord Keeper and Lord Chancellor, reversed his decree. North evidently felt that Lord Nottingham had given the perpetuity rule a dangerous elasticity in the Chancery, for he indulges in an outburst against perpetuities which indicates that he was prepared to preserve all the more restrictive characteristics of the older rules. He says—

> A perpetuity is a thing odious in law, and destructive to the commonwealth: it would put a stop to commerce and prevent the circulation of the riches of the kingdom; and therefore is not to be countenanced in equity. If in equity you could come nearer to a perpetuity than the rules of common law would admit, all men, being desirous to continue their estates, in their families, would settle their estates by way of trust: which might indeed make well for the jurisdiction of the court, but would be destructive to the commonwealth.

This, however, was exactly what Lord Nottingham's rule prevented, and therefore the House of Lords, in 1685, restored Lord Nottingham's decree, after two days' argument, in a full House, without a division.

The *Duke of Norfolk's* case, in reality, was not so much a rule as a principle, capable of progressive extension. It simply held that limitations which take effect within lives in being are good, and it completely rejected an attempted distinction between terms of years and freehold interests from this point of view. The gradual development of the rule to its modern proportions is very plainly described by Hargrave in his argument in *Thellusson* v. *Woodford.* The main points may be summarised as follows—

(1) In *Snow* v. *Cutler* "a devise to the heirs of the body of the devisor's wife, if they should attain the age of fourteen, was warmly contested upon the ground of being an executory devise to a person not *in esse*, and a contingency upon a contingency: viz. the birth of a child, and its attaining fourteen: but I do not observe, that the mere circumstance of fourteen years beyond a life in being was much objected to."

(2) In *Lloyd* v. *Carew* a limitation which took effect twelve months after lives in being was held good.

(3) In *Scattergood* v. *Edge*, the question whether a life or lives in being was the extreme limit was still an open one.

(4) However, in *Stephens* v. *Stephens* an executory devise to an unborn child of a living person at twenty-one was held good. This, with the addition of the period of gestation in appropriate cases, set the boundary, in terms of time for the modern rule, although it remained for still later cases to decide that any life in being, and not simply the lives of those with interests under the settlement might be selected.

As Professor Plucknett has remarked—

> Inconveniences have arisen, and the growing rule received its due measure of complications and difficulties, but it is thanks to Lord Nottingham's courage and perception that the rule has as its basis a reasonable and simple proposition, instead of the artificial complications which the common law courts had been devising in order to meet the problem.[1]

It was perhaps, inevitable that the rule, once enunciated, should be developed with increasing technicality, though there can be little question that Lord Nottingham would have been surprised at some of the later applications of the doctrine. A number of these have been considered by the Law Reform Committee, and it will therefore be convenient to consider them in connection with the Report of that Committee.

To sum up, therefore, the Perpetuity Rule provides—

No interest is good unless it must vest, if at all, not later than twenty-one years after some life in being at the creation of the interest.[2]

The Rule, it will be perceived, applies to the vesting of interests, and not to their duration. By "vesting" is meant that the persons who will take the interest are ascertained, and that such persons are ready to take, without any prior condition being satisfied, as soon as the preceding interest ends. To this it should be added that a class gift is not "vested" until the membership of the class is ascertained. This factor, hazy in the past, created many difficult problems.

[1] *Concise History of the Common Law*, 5th Ed., p. 598.
[2] Gray, *Perpetuities*, 4th Ed., S. 201.

2. Is there a Rule Against Inalienability?

Before dealing with the recommendations in the Report which are concerned with the Perpetuity Rule properly so called, it will be valuable to dispose first of a modern heresy which has increasingly found a place in judicial pronouncements during the past century. The Rule, if it exists, is mainly associated with the problems which arise in respect of attempts to create trusts for non-human beneficiaries. The literature on this topic is extensive,[1] but the problem can be resolved into two questions—

1. Can there be a trust for non-human beneficiaries, where the object of the trust is non-charitable?

2. If there can be such a trust, what is the maximum duration which the law will allow to it?

On the first head, there has been remarkably little discussion of general principles. For the most part, the argument has turned upon the new meaning of certain observations of Grant, M.R., in *Morice* v. *Bishop of Durham*. They are as follows—

> There can be no trust over which this Court will not assume control; for an uncontrollable power of disposition would be ownership and not trust. If there be a clear trust, but for uncertain objects, the property that is the subject of the trust is undisposed of; and the benefit of such trust must result to those to whom the law gives the ownership in default of disposition by the former owner. But this doctrine does not hold with regard to trusts for clients. Every other trust must have a definite object. There must be somebody in whose favour the Court can decree performance.

Unless the entire argument is to be built upon the single word *somebody*, this looks like nothing more than a reference to the three certainties of a trust, and an assertion that the objects of a trust must be certain, and this impression is confirmed by reference to the case itself. It arose upon a direction in a will that the residue of an estate should be distributed amongst such objects of benevolence and liberality as the Bishop of Durham, as executor, should approve. It has long ago been decided that the word "benevolent" is wider than

[1] For references, see Morris and Barton Leach, p. 295.

charitable, and accordingly, where this word is used to define the objects of distribution the gift fails for uncertainty. The Master of the Rolls expressly says at the beginning of his judgment that "the only question is, whether the trust, upon which the residue of the personal estate is bequeathed, be a trust for a charitable purpose." It seems strange, therefore, that this case has been frequently cited as authority in cases where the object of the trust is quite certain, but is not a charity and is also non-human.

Indeed, the only way in which such dispositions by way of trust can be discussed is from the standpoint of broad principle and public policy. It may be technically unassailable for a settlor or testator to devote large sums of money to the maintenance of a monument for a long period, but is this such an object that the law will desire to see achieved? This aspect of the question received consideration by Roxburgh, J., in *Re Astor's Settlement Trusts*, in the course of a highly interesting judgment, in which he reviewed the earlier authorities. The Astor trust had moved one stage further towards indefiniteness, for it was concerned, not with tangible objects, such as monuments or animals, but with the effectuation of certain purposes specified in the trust deed. Roxburgh, J., thought that the trusts in any case failed for uncertainty but he was also of opinion that the earlier decisions relating to tangible non-human objects should not be extended to abstract purposes. He goes to the root of the matter in saying—

> If the purposes are not charitable, great difficulties arise both in theory and in practice. In theory, because having regard to the historical origins of equity it is difficult to visualise the growth of equitable obligations which nobody can enforce, and in practice, because it is not possible to contemplate with equanimity the creation of large funds devoted to non-charitable purposes which no court and no department of state can control, or, in the case of maladministration, reform. Therefore Lord Parker's second proposition[1] would *prima facie* appear to be well-founded. Moreover it gains no little support from the practical considerations that no officer has ever been constituted to take, in the case of non-charitable purposes, the position held by the Attorney-General

[1] In *Bowman* v. *Secular Society, Ltd.*, the second proposition was that a trust to be valid must either be for individuals or a charity.

> in connection with charitable purposes, and no case has been found in the reports in which the Court has ever directly enforced a non-charitable purpose against a trustee. Indeed, where, as in the present case, the only beneficiaries are purposes and an at present unascertainable person, it is difficult to see who could initiate such proceedings. If the purposes are valid trusts, the settlors have retained no beneficial interest and could not initiate them. It was suggested that the trustees might proceed *ex parte* to enforce the trusts against themselves. I doubt that, but at any rate nobody could enforce the trusts against them. This point, in my judgment, is of importance, because in most of the cases which are put forward to disprove Lord Parker's propositions the Court had indirect meaning of enforcing the executors of the non-charitable trusts.

This last situation could arise, for example, if the residuary legatee claimed the property on the ground that the trustees were failing to execute the trust.

In *Re Dean*, North, J., put forward the view that there may be a trust for a monument or for animals in the following terms—

> There it is said, that there is no *cestui que trust* who can enforce the trust, and that the Court will not recognise a trust unless it is capable of being enforced by someone. I do not assent to this view. There is not the least doubt that a man may if he pleases, give a legacy to trustees, upon trust to apply it in erecting a monument to himself, either in a church or in a churchyard, or even in unconsecrated ground, and I am not aware that such a trust is in any way invalid, although it is difficult to say who would be the *cestui que trust* of the monument. In the same way I know of nothing to prevent a gift of a sum of money to trustees, upon trust to apply it for the repair of such a monument. In my opinion such a trust would be good, although the testator must be careful to limit the time for which it is to last, because as it is not a charitable trust, unless it is to come to an end within the limits fixed by the rule against perpetuities, it would be illegal. But a trust to lay out a certain sum in building a monument, and the gift of another sum in trust to apply the same to keeping that monument in repair, say, for ten years, is, in my opinion, a perfectly good trust, although I do not see who could ask the court to enforce it.

Reviewing the earlier cases in *Re Astor's Settlement*, therefore, Roxburgh, J., accepted these earlier decisions as anomalous and exceptional. They extend to horses and dogs, graves and monuments, and are matters arising under wills and intimately connected with the deceased, which cannot "justify the conclusion that a Court of Equity will recognise as an equitable obligation affecting the income of large funds in the hands of trustees a direction to apply it in furtherance of enumerated non-charitable purposes in a manner which no court or department can control or enforce."

The observations of North, J., in *Re Dean* contain a second difficulty, which has never been satisfactorily resolved. He says that the trust for non-human objects would be good for the perpetuity period. What exactly is meant by this? The perpetuity rule, it has been shown, was evolved to regulate the vesting of interests, but North, J., is here using the term to cover their duration. Moreover, by "the perpetuity period" the courts have meant a period of approximately twenty-one years.[1] There seems to be no case in which the courts have been called upon to consider such a trust for monuments or animals, limited to last for a life in being and twenty-one years thereafter. Such a limitation might have caused the Court some embarrassment. In the Astor Settlement, however, this period was actually selected, but there is no evidence that it influenced Roxburgh, J., to hold the trusts invalid.

The Report of the Law Reform Committee accepted the position that trusts within the limits set by Roxburgh, J., in *Re Astor's Settlement* are valid, but it proposes that any settlor shall be able to devote a sum of the order of £1,000 to a perpetual trust, the income of which may be applied in perpetuity to maintain a grave, tomb or monument, either with or without power to resort to capital.[2] This recommendation, it may be hoped, will render obsolete the learning which has accumulated around—

(1) *Re Tyler* and *Re Dalziel*, when the device of a gift over from one charity to another was used, upon condition that the first charity maintained the testator's grave. The second case made it clear that if this device is used, the income to be used in maintenance of the grave should not be derived from

[1] *Pirbright* v. *Salwey; Re Elliott.* [2] Paras. 49–53.

the income enjoyed by the first charity, otherwise the whole gift fails; and

(2) *Re Chardon*, in which there was a gift of the income of a fund to a non-charitable cemetery company "so long as it maintained the testator's grave." This gift was held good, on the ground that it vested immediately, so that no question of perpetuity arose. The case has provoked prolonged discussion upon the possibility of creating determinable interests in personalty, but is also remarkable for the strange views which were expressed in argument upon the effects of the Rule against Perpetuities.

3. The Report of the Law Reform Committee

The Law Reform Committee's Fourth Report on the Rule against Perpetuities[1] appeared in November 1956. Since Dr. J. H. C. Morris was a member of the sub-committee which reported to the main committee upon the state of the law, it is not surprising that a number of the recommendations eventually made reflect the views expressed by Dr. Morris and Professor Barton Leach. In making such recommendations for change, however, it may be that Dr. Morris, and the Law Reform Committee have minimised the importance of the conclusions to be drawn from American experience by Dr. Morris and Professor Barton Leach, which was mentioned at the beginning of this chapter. Nevertheless, it might fairly be said that the recommendations of the Committee do not suggest any alteration of major principles, but simply the modification of a number of specific points. In so far as the perpetuity period itself is concerned, the Committee suggested that, in place of the lives in being and twenty-one years after, the settlor may select, if he pleases, a straight period of years not exceeding eighty.

Two other recommendations are designed to remove absurdities which have been imported into the decisions, affecting the age of child-bearing. In *Jee* v. *Audley* a limitation was held void for perpetuity on the ridiculous ground that a woman, then turned seventy years of age, might have another

[1] Cmnd. 18.

child. Unfortunately, this decision had been consistently followed, more especially in *Re Dawson* where the woman was nearly fifty-two years of age at the date of the will under which the limitation arose, and more than sixty years of age at the date of the testator's death. In that case Chitty, J., reviewed the earlier authorities, and pointed out that Lord Brougham in *Dungannon* v. *Smith* had described Lord Kenyon's decision in *Jee* v. *Audley* as one of the landmarks of the law. Prehistoric survival might have been an apter term, and it is perhaps not surprising that Chitty, J., cites a particularly ponderous observation of Coke in support of it.

More recently the courts have toyed with the problem at the other extreme. In *Re Gaite* the testatrix directed her trustees to pay the income of £500 to Mrs. Hagar Gaite for life, and after her death to stand possessed of the income and capital in trust for such of her grandchildren living at the textatrix's death or born within five years therefrom who shall attain the age of twenty-one or being a woman shall marry under that age, and she bequeathed a share of residue on similar trusts. The question was raised whether the reversionary trusts of the legacy infringed the perpetuity rule. Roxburgh, J., pointed out that Mrs. Hagar Gaite, who was alive at the date of the death of the testatrix might have had a child within five years of the death of the testatrix and that such a child should marry and have a child within five years. He said—

> I do not base my judgment upon physical impossibility. I leave all questions of that sort open for consideration when they arise[1] because the matter is, in my judgment, concluded by the Age of Marriage Act, 1929, which provides by Sect. 1: "A marriage between persons either of whom is under the age of sixteen shall be void".

However, the possibility which the learned judge mentioned was sufficient to induce the Law Reform Committee to make a recommendation in respect of it. It has therefore recommended that there should be rebuttable presumptions: (i) that no woman who has obtained the age of fifty-five shall be deemed capable of childbearing; and (ii) that no male or

[1] Presumably in a less extreme case.

female who has not attained the age of fourteen shall be deemed capable of procreating or bearing a child. It is provided, however, as a safeguard, that any decision based on these presumptions shall not be invalidated by the subsequent birth of a child, nor will it debar the child from taking under any limitation which is not void for perpetuity.[1]

The Report also tackles the problem of class gifts. Here, as has been noticed, difficulties often arise because a class may only be closed outside the permitted period, in which case the gift to the whole class fails. The Committee therefore recommend that such gifts should be good in so far as those who qualify within the permitted period are concerned. The Report also recommends that where in a limitation there is a gift to A, with remainder to any widow he may leave, and then to such children as may survive A and his widow, such limitations shall henceforth not fail simply because the wife of A may not be born at the time when the instrument takes effect.[2] Limitations have frequently failed on this ground in the past.[3]

The Report seeks to remove another tiresome technicality by providing that a limitation which is within the Rule should not fail simply because it follows some invalid limitation, whether or not the subsequent limitation is dependent upon the invalid prior limitation. In such a case, if the earlier limitation is invalid, the subsequent one will be accelerated.[4] Under the present law, any limitation which is dependent or expectant upon a prior limitation which is void for remoteness fails.[5]

The Report also suggests modifications of the Rule in its application to powers of appointment. In so far as general powers are concerned, these have been regarded as equivalent to a right of property in the donor of the power. Accordingly the perpetuity period dates from the actual appointment, and not from the date when the power was given. This is so whether the power is exercisable by deed or will. The rule, however, is not applicable where the power is a joint one, or

[1] Paras. 11–13. [2] Para. 28.
[3] See Morris and Barton Leach, pp. 70–71.
[4] Paras. 32–33.
[5] See *Re Abbott; Re Canning's Will Trusts; Re Coleman.*

where it can only be exercised with the consent of another.[1] Where a special power of appointment is given, however, the perpetuity period runs from the date when the power is given, not from the date when it is exercised. The Committee adopts the view which prevailed in *Re Churston's Settled Estates*, and recommends that all powers should be regarded as special, unless the power is to be exercised by a sole donee who can at any moment appoint himself, subject to the qualification that an appointment made by will may be regarded as a general power.

The Committee also make certain recommendations intended to vary the orbit of the rule. They would exclude the powers of trustees to sell, lease or dispose of property where they are ancillary to valid subsisting trusts,[2] options in leases[3] and rights of entry exercisable in respect of rent charges.[4] On the other hand, it is suggested that possibilities of reverter and resulting trusts of personalty analogous to such possibilities should be within the perpetuity rule.[5] The effect of this would be that unless the event on which the prior interest determined occurred within the perpetuity period, the prior interest would become absolute, and the possibility or resulting trust would fail. These recommendations, if adopted, would have the merit of ending a highly technical controversy, on which the authorities are remarkably obscure.[6]

[1] See *Re Churston's Settled Estates*.
[2] Para. 34.
[3] Paras. 35–7.
[4] Paras. 42–3.
[5] Paras. 39–41.
[6] See Morris and Barton Leach, pp. 203 *et seqq*.

CHAPTER IV

The Will of Peter Thellusson

FOR some inexplicable reason the will of Peter Thellusson rarely fails to provoke the ire of legal writers. By a progressive legal fiction, Thellusson has become a species of legal monster, upon which it is safe for student and teacher alike to vent their animosity. Thus, in the middle of a calm exposition of the Rule against Perpetuities, the authors of a most excellent volume on perpetuities[1] suddenly comment that "it failed to invalidate the most notoriously eccentric and anti-social dispositions that ever came before the courts—those of Peter Thellusson."[2] Later on, in discussing the *Thellusson* case more fully, they add: "Peter Thellusson thus locked his treasure in a mausoleum and flung the key to some remote descendant yet unborn, regardless of the claims which his wife and children might have had upon his bounty."[3] Neither of these statements accurately describes the will, although it has been the fashion to describe it in similar terms ever since his family and contemporaries imputed to it "injustice, absurdity, eccentricity, ambition, avarice and heartlessness." Thellusson's contemporaries, however, were startled by the possibilities which this ingenious piece of conveyancing opened up, and it seems probable, from the evidence of the will itself, that lawyers and politicians had been gossiping about it even during his lifetime, for he says in it: "As I have earned the fortune which I now possess with industry and honesty, I trust and hope that the legislature will not in any manner alter my will or the limitations thereby created, but permit my property to go in the manner in which I hereby dispose of it." This was

[1] *The Rule Against Perpetuities*, by J. H. C. Morris and W. Barton Leach.
[2] P. 15.
[3] P. 259.

not eccentricity, but well-founded suspicion, for the Thellusson Act was hastily rushed through Parliament in 1800, although it was not given retrospective operation to Thellusson's will. Surely after a century and a half it is now time that we freed ourselves of the prejudices of Thellusson's contemporaries, based as they were upon fantastic forebodings upon the effects of long accumulations. Unfortunately, one looks in vain in the textbooks for any true estimate of one of the most celebrated wills in English legal history. It will therefore be valuable to set out its main provisions somewhat fully, for, contrary to the impression given by most textbooks, the famous accumulations clause did not apply to the whole of Thellusson's estate, but only to a part of it.

1. The Thellusson Will[1]

Peter Thellusson was a West India merchant of Huguenot extraction, who had accumulated a considerable fortune. He died on 21st July, 1797, having made the will about which all the controversy arose just over a year earlier, on 2nd April, 1796. His age is not stated in the report, but it was evidently substantial, for he left a number of grandchildren. Moreover, there is evidence in the will that his sons had been associated with him in the West India trade for a number of years, the eldest being thirty-six years of age at the time of Peter Thellusson's death.

In order to make clear the problem arising under the will, it will be convenient to set out the family in a genealogical table—

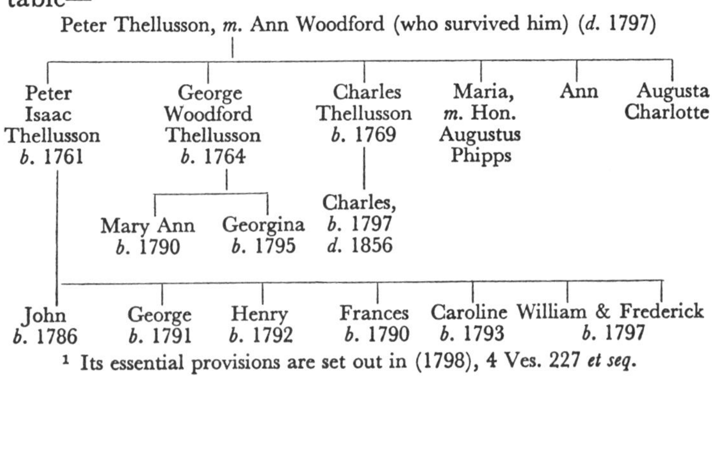

[1] Its essential provisions are set out in (1798), 4 Ves. 227 *et seq.*

The widow, Ann, appears to have been a Woodford, and a member of a large family. In his will Peter Thellusson appoints as trustees two brothers-in-law, the Rev. Matthew Woodford and the curiously-named Emperor John Alexander Woodford, together with James Stanley, whilst elsewhere he gives legacies of a hundred guineas each to two nephews, who are described as nephews, being sons of Colonel Woodford, who was presumably another brother-in-law.

The will, though lengthy, was clear and logical. After directing the payment of his debts and general expenses, he left legacies of 300 guineas to each of his executors. He then made provision for his widow. She was to be paid 300 guineas ten days after his death, together with such plate as she should choose to the amount of 1,400 ounces, in addition to all the jewellery in her possession. She was also to occupy for life or until re-marriage, the testator's house at Plaistow, where they had been living, together with all its furniture, horses, cattle, carriages and implements of husbandry. The testator then directed that a fund should be created, out of which the widow was to receive £2,140 a year for life, which was to be reduced on her re-marriage. On the death of the widow, this fund, comprising £22,000 Bank Stock and £600 a year Long Annuities, was to be divided as follows: £4,000 Bank Stock to each of his three sons, £1,500 Bank Stock to each of his three daughters, and the Long Annuities were to be divided equally between the three daughters. The remaining £5,500 Bank Stock was also given to his sons and daughters in such shares as his widow should appoint, and in default of appointment to his children in equal shares.

Each of the sons was then given £7,600 "to make the money already advanced to them £23,000 each," and in addition Peter and George received a small annuity on their lives in the French funds, and Charles an annuity on his life in the Irish Tontine. Evidently the testator had been generous to his sons during his lifetime—a fact which appears in a later part of the will. Each of them had been associated with him in his immensely profitable business, as well as receiving very substantial cash portions. After his death, they were to continue to occupy his business premises in Philpot Lane, in order to carry on the business, which had now become theirs. Each of them was already a wealthy man, as a result of their father's enterprise, allied with their own efforts, for the testator says in his will—

> . . . The provision which I have made for my said three sons, and the very great success they have met with, will be sufficient to procure them comfort; and it is my earnest wish and desire that they will avoid ostentation, vanity and pompous show; and that will be the best fortune they can possess.

To return to his provision for the family, the testator left £100 Irish Tontine to his eldest daughter, and various life annuities in the French funds to each of the three daughters, and various other annuities to John, the eldest son of the testator's eldest son, Peter Isaac; and certain other annuities to his two nephews, the sons of Colonel Woodford, who also received legacies of £105 at twenty-one. Finally, there are gifts of rings to the value of £50 to each of his three daughters-in-law and to his son-in-law, and a legacy of £1,000 in trust for his brother for life, and after the brother's death, for the brother's daughter.

Following this not illiberal provision for a large family comes the famous bequest of the residue, estimated to exceed £600,000, to his executors and trustees to accumulate during the lives of his sons and grandsons living at his death, and at the expiration of this period to convey the fund in equal third lots in tail male to the eldest lineal male descendant of each of his three sons, with an ultimate remainder, on failure of male lineal descendants, to the Crown to be used as a sinking fund, as directed by Act of Parliament, *i.e.* to reduce the National Debt. The will also contains a grant of wide powers of leasing and management to the trustees.

The limitation, it will be seen, provided that this estate was to vest within the perpetuity period, and there being at that time no Accumulations Act, the period of accumulation was not excessive. Accordingly, Lord Chancellor Loughborough, after consulting the Master of the Rolls and two common law judges, Buller and Lawrence, held the bequest good, and their decision was confirmed by the House of Lords (which then included Lord Chancellor Eldon) six years later. There could be no doubt that at that date accumulations could be directed for the full perpetuity period. The surprising thing was that fuller advantage had not been taken of this state of affairs, although in *Webb* v. *Earl of Shaftesbury*, in the same year, an accumulation of £10,000 for approximately seventy years was directed. The anxieties which the case provoked, though partly due to the disappointment of the expectations of the Thellusson family, was mainly due to the almost superstitious fear of the power of compound interest which then existed. The amount of the fund, when fully matured by accumulation, was variously estimated as 19 millions, 30 millions, or even 100 millions. Whatever it might be it was not thought to be a good thing to encourage such accumulations of capital. This was before the days of limited liability, when the existence of such funds, operating in trade, industry or finance is commonplace.

What Peter Thellusson intended to do was clear enough. He was a trader who had prospered, and so had his family. After making proper provision for that family, he wanted to "make an heir," or rather, three heirs, possibly with the further ambition that one of these ultimate heirs should grace the House of Lords.[1] This, in fact, occurred, as Peter Isaac Thellusson reached the House of Lords as Lord Rendlesham. This was the commonest aspiration of the trading class at that period, and even among the upper classes, the desire to obtain a peerage, or a higher rank in the peerage, was practically universal. In *Egerton* v. *Earl Brownlow*, a contingent remainder was limited to vest upon the legatee obtaining the title of marquis or duke. Thellusson's will was better drawn and less objectionable in objective.

The *Thellusson* case attracted very considerable attention, and much controversy whilst it was going through the courts. Before the House of Lords had disposed of the appeal, Parliament had passed the Accumulations Act, 1800, limiting the possible periods of accumulation. This Act was re-enacted in Sect. 164 of the Law of Property Act, 1925. But it is a little difficult, at this date, to discover what all the excitement was about. Mr. Hargrave, as might be expected, in attacking the

[1] Bramwell, B., makes this suggestion in *Thellusson* v. *Rendlesham*.

will before Lord Loughborough, used the hoary fallacy that to uphold the will would have the result "that executory devise may be applied to prevent all alienation of property for 120 or even 140 years; and by combining with it accumulation it may be possible to prohibit all beneficial enjoyment during the same period. Such a combination of trust of accumulation with executory devise would not be endured without the most glaring and dangerous mischief to the community by locking up an immense property and the income of it for many years to the great injury of commerce"—and so forth. The will did nothing of the sort. The fund was there, and the trustees were given powers to manage it. Land could be occupied and enjoyed, money was invested, exactly as if it was beneficially enjoyed. The only difference, apart from that between the position of a trustee and the position of a beneficial owner, was that the Thellusson family's expectations were defeated in favour of a remoter descendant. Moreover, counsel for the trustees and for the Crown put the matter in a nutshell, when they said: "Accumulation may happen in the ordinary case. Suppose the trust was to convey to a son of the testator's infant son; then that son dies leaving an infant son; this Court in its ordinary jurisdiction would accumulate the rents and profits; and must do so, if the necessity of the accumulation should continue for two centuries."

It scarcely needs to be pointed out that when unclaimed estates remain in the custody of the Chancery Division over long periods, this is exactly what occurs. It is, however, possible to go further, and to show that the Accumulations Act, 1800, very nearly failed in its primary object. Suppose that a will were to be made, containing a clause similar to that which appeared in Thellusson's will, but without the accumulations clause. What would happen to the income in the interval between the testator's death and the time when the property vests, bearing in mind that the income of residue is itself residue? This was the problem discussed in *Tench* v. *Cheese*. Dr. Morris and Professor Leach refer to this very problem in their book, where they say (p. 266)—

> It was at one time supposed that the Act applied only to an express direction to accumulate: but this doctrine is now ex-

> ploded. If this were not so, some future Thellusson could attain his ends by bequeathing his property to his eldest male descendant living at the death of the surviving *cestuis que vie*, and merely omitting the direction to accumulate.

In *Tench* v. *Cheese* the Master of the Rolls, in a full and learned judgment, held the implied accumulation good as occurring by operation of law, and there are obviously strong arguments which can be advanced to support this view. However, on appeal, the full Court of Appeal in Chancery decided otherwise, and the Lord Chancellor, who delivered the leading judgment said of the Accumulations Act—

> We have to deal with one of the most ill-drawn statutes, perhaps, that is to be found in the Statute Book. It is rather singular it should be so, because it is well-known it was introduced in consequence of a very important will—Thellusson's will. The act was brought in under the sanction of the Lord Chancellor of that day, and it underwent great discussion. No doubt it was very much considered, every one feeling the importance of the subject, and the Act, as we all very well know, was called "Thellusson's Act". Although it was an Act that received very great consideration, it unfortunately is framed in such very obscure language that it is exceedingly difficult to apply it to the different cases which from time to time arise.

Actually, in *Tench* v. *Cheese*, the Court of Appeal in Chancery were able to satisfy themselves that the will was cast in such a form that they could spell out from it an express direction to accumulate. However, in other cases, it was settled that where the vesting of interests is postponed beyond the perpetuity period, and the gift carries the intermediate income, then the accumulation is limited to one of the specified periods. In *Re Taylor*, Cozens-Hardy, J., makes the interesting observation—

> Since *Hodgson* v. *Bective*, 10 H.L.C. 656, and I think for a long period before that decision, it has been settled law that a gift of personalty contingently to a class carries with it the intermediate income not disposed of. Originally it carried with it the intermediate income during the whole period allowed for the suspension of vesting, a period which has since been shortened by the Accumulations Act, 1800.

Today, therefore, where the vesting of the residue is postponed within the perpetuity period, there is an accumulation for the permitted period, and after that there is an intestacy as to the excess income.

2. The Later History of the Thellusson Will

When Thellusson drew up his will in 1796, he might reasonably have expected that the final distribution should occur some time between 1870 and 1880. In fact, it took place in 1856, for on 5th February of that year, Charles Thellusson, son of Charles, the testator's youngest son, died. Charles the younger, who was born in 1797, was, surprisingly, the last survivor of the testator's sons, and such of their sons as were living or *en ventre sa mère* at the time of the testator's death. Moreover, the anticipations of those who expected the fortune, even during this period of accumulation, to have reached sensational proportions, were sadly disappointed. The will was constantly before the courts, and all possible parties were represented lavishly, in the comfortable knowledge that all expenses would be met out of the estate. Appeals were lodged with monotonous regularity, with the result that the will became almost as familiar to the House of Lords as that of Lord St. Leonards was at a later date. Yet few of these cases raise points of importance, and some are concerned with details of administration. The only two of major importance were the first, in which first the Lord Chancellor, and later the House of Lords, decided in favour of the validity of the accumulation, and the last, which settled the destination of what remained of the fund. Surveying this long line of decisions, it is impossible to acquit the family of Peter Thellusson, and also his trustees, of a capriciousness that they ascribed to him. This impression is strengthened by recalling that in the early part of the nineteenth century the family unsuccessfully promoted numerous petitions to Parliament to have the will altered, and the period of distribution hastened. Finally, in 1833, the trustees of the will promoted a private Act of Parliament, "for enabling and directing the trustees of the will of Peter Thellusson Esquire, deceased, to grant certain leases of the estates subject to the trusts of the said will; and for other purposes." All these proceedings no doubt brought joy to the legal profession. They would have appalled the testator.

When the time for partition of the fund arrived, the family was strikingly changed from what it had been at the time of Peter Thellusson's death. Peter's eldest son, Peter Isaac, had duly reached the peerage as the first Baron Rendlesham. The first three sons of Peter Isaac had all died without male issue, before reaching middle age, for Frederick, one of the twins born in 1797, shortly after their grandfather's death, was the third Lord Rendlesham. He, too, died early, and the respondent in *Thellusson* v. *Rendelsham* in 1858 was his only son, born in 1840, who was thus the fourth Lord Rendlesham.

At the time of partition, there were no male lineal descendants of the testator's second son, George Woodford Thellusson, and under the terms of the will, the trust property was therefore to be divided into two lots, between the "eldest male lineal descendant" of Peter Isaac, and the "eldest male lineal descendant" of Charles, but for the other half-share, there were two claimants, the fourth Lord Rendlesham, and the appellant, his uncle, who was a younger son of the third Lord Rendlesham, but who was considerably older than his nephew. The uncle contended that he was entitled to the half-share of the fund, as he was the male lineal descendant of Peter Isaac, who was the eldest in age. The fourth Lord Rendlesham contended that the words of the will meant that the person entitled was the senior male representative in the male line, *i.e.* himself, and the Master of the Rolls, and the House of Lords (after consultation with the judiciary) agreed with him. The report shows that the case was twice argued on appeal before the House of Lords—on three days in July 1858, and on four days in February 1859. Much learning appears to have been expended upon a point which seems blatantly obvious, although once again there was the comfortable assurance that old Peter Thellusson was paying. This, however, was the last act of the Thellusson will drama. With the fund at last divided, there was nothing left for his descendants to litigate about, and thenceforth, there was no estate to pay costs.

Looking back, it is extraordinarily difficult to discover why Thellusson has been treated so shabbily by textbook writers. His object in making the will was clear, and was shared by many of his contemporaries. He provided adequately for all his family before directing an accumulation which was lawful, and which was a logical development from others in wills of approximately the same period. The will was clear and well-drawn; indeed this was frequently commented on by the judges who considered it, and some of the litigation in which it figured (including the last case of all) seems somewhat frivolous or, alternatively, is an illustration of the bad feeling which existed between various branches of the testator's descendants. Perhaps it is not too late even now to correct the common misunderstanding of Peter Thellusson. If anyone in the Thellusson story was unreasonable, it is difficult to conclude that it was the testator.

3. The Modern Rule Against Accumulations

Peter Thellusson's will produced the Accumulations Act, 1800, which was re-enacted in Sect. 164 of the Law of Property Act, 1925. At various times since that date, the provisions of the Act have been extended to Scotland, Ireland, Australia, New Zealand and most of the Canadian provinces.[1] This is a little surprising, since the Act itself shows the marks of hasty drafting, and nearly failed in one of its main objects, where accumulation was implied, as has already been pointed out. The act establishes four alternative periods of accumulation.[2] These are:

1. The life of the settlor;
2. a term of twenty-one years from the death of the grantor or settlor;
3. the duration of the minority or respective minorities of any person or persons living or *en ventre sa mère* at the death of the settlor;
4. the duration of the minority or respective minorities only of any person or persons who under the limitations of the instrument directing the accumulations would, for the time

[1] Morris and Barton Leach, pp. 260–1.

[2] Certain exceptions exist. Law of Property Act, 1925, Sect. 164 (2).

being, if of full age, be entitled to the income directed to be accumulated.

To these four periods, the Law Reform Committee have recently recommended that two additional periods shall be added, applicable to settlements *inter vivos*. They are: (1) twenty-one years from the date of the settlement, and (2) the minority or respective minorities of any persons living or *en ventre* at that date.[1] The periods are alternative, and only one may be chosen.[2] The interest period to which accumulation can be directed under the Act is, for practical purposes, twenty-one years, for only an unusual combination of circumstances could produce a period longer by a few months under (3) and under (4) although there might be successive accumulations, it would be most unusual for them to follow immediately upon one another, and indeed, none of them may arise at all, if the beneficiaries are of full age when they receive their interests. The first period is, of course, applicable only to instruments *inter vivos*, and the settlor in such a case does no more than direct what he could himself have done with his own property in any case. Moreover, in such a case, there is not even the possibility of escaping death duty, for where an accumulation is directed for the life of the settlor, property passes on his death within the meaning of Sect. 1 of the Finance Act, 1894.[3]

When an excessive accumulation is directed, then the direction is totally void if it directed an accumulation for a period exceeding the perpetuity period, but it is void for excess only where the direction is within the perpetuity period but exceeds what is permitted under the Act.[4]

An important point on the relation of the provisions for accumulation in Sect. 164 of the Law of Property Act, 1925, to provisions for accumulation of surplus income during an infant's minority under (what is now) Sect. 31 of the Trustee Act, 1925, was decided in *Re Maber*. If, when a period of accumulation under the Law of Property Act, 1925, has been completed, there is a minority, with power to maintain the infant under Sect. 31 of the Trustee Act, 1925, an accumu-

[1] Cmnd. 18, paras. 56–7.
[2] *Jagger* v. *Jagger*.
[3] *Re Bourne's Settlement*.
[4] *Re Rosslyn's Trust; Re Blake*.

lation of surplus income for the infant's eventual benefit takes place. This is, indeed, expressly provided in Sect. 165 of the Law of Property Act, 1925.

Although Sect. 165 and *Re Maber* may be taken to have settled the question of successive or overlapping accumulations under the two statutes there remains the distinct, but associated, problem which occurs when an accumulation under Sect. 164 has been directed, for a beneficiary who is an infant whilst the accumulation is taking place, whether he can be maintained out of the income which is being accumulated. In such a case, if there is an express direction to accumulate, maintenance out of income is excluded,[1] but not where the trust for accumulation is implied.[2]

In the great majority of cases today, the problem of maintenance in settlements is of importance chiefly in respect of the interests of infant beneficiaries. In such cases, therefore, an express direction to accumulate may defeat the possibility of maintenance. On the other hand, where the infant beneficiary is entitled to the intermediate income, the Trustee Act, 1925, Sect. 31, will itself direct the accumulation of surplus income. Accordingly, a settlor may perhaps be forgiven for wondering whether Sect. 154 is of any great value, or whether it is better to avoid it altogether.

One further point relating to accumulation remained for a long time in a state of uncertainty, viz. whether the Rule applied both to accumulations at compound and simple interest. The Report of the Law Reform Committee has now recommended that the Rule should apply to both types of accumulation, and also to powers to accumulate.

[1] *Re Reade-Revell.* [2] *Re Leng.*

CHAPTER V

Remoulding Beneficial Interests in Trusts

THE decision of the House of Lords in *Chapman* v. *Chapman* temporarily checked a movement to bring the Law of Trusts in practice a little more into harmony with the changed conditions of the mid-twentieth century. Indeed, its restrictive effect produced so much criticism that a Committee to enquire into effects was promptly constituted.

When *Chapman* v. *Chapman* was considered by the Court of Appeal, it was one of three appeals which were considered together. All three had certain common features, but there were also differences between them. The principal common feature was that, if the Court was able to assent to the scheme put before it in each case, a substantial sum in death duties could be avoided. The *Chapman* appeal related to three settlements. By the first, Colonel Sir Robert Chapman and his wife, Lady Chapman, settled land or the proceeds of sale thereof and other property. Clauses 2, 3 and 4 of the settlement read as follows—

> 2. The trustees shall stand possessed of the trust premises (subject to clauses 3 and 4 following) for all or any the child or children of the settlors' son Robert Macgowran Chapman who shall attain the age of 21 years or die under that age leaving issue and if more than one in equal shares as tenants in common.
>
> 3. Provided always that until the youngest child of the said Robert Macgowran Chapman shall have attained the age of 25 years if that event shall happen within 21 years from the date hereof or until the expiration of 21 years from the death of the survivor of the settlors if the youngest surviving child of the said Robert Macgowran Chapman shall not then have attained the age of 25 years the trustees shall retain the trust premises and shall apply such part as they in their discretion shall think fit of the income thereof for or towards common maintenance education or other benefits of the children of the

said Robert Macgowran Chapman for the time being living whether minors or adults or for or towards the maintenance education or other benefit of any one or more of them to the exclusion of the other or others and shall (subject as hereinafter mentioned) accumulate the surplus of such income until the time for distribution by investing the same and the resulting income thereof in any investments hereby authorised in augmentation of the capital of the trust premises to be held upon the same trust as the original trust premises but so that the trustees may apply accumulation of any preceding year or years in or towards the maintenance education or benefit of all or any of the said children in the same manner as such accumulations might have been applied had they been income arising from the original trust funds in the then current year.

Provided always that after each child of the said Robert Macgowran Chapman has attained his or her majority the surplus income of his share in the trust premises not expended by virtue of the foregoing powers of this clause shall not be accumulated but shall be paid to such child.

4. Provided also that the trustees may at any time with the consent in writing of the settlors raise any part or parts not exceeding in the whole one half of the then expectant or presumptive or vested share of any child whether minor or adult of the said Robert Macgowran Chapman on the trust premises under the trust hereinbefore contained and pay or apply the same to him or her for his or her advancement or otherwise for his or her exclusive benefit in such manner as the trustees shall think fit and as to the part or parts so raised the maintenance and other trusts of the last preceding clause shall cease to be applicable and no interest on any such advance shall be charged to any child so advanced in the accounts of the trust.

In the second settlement, dated 8th February, 1950, Lady Chapman settled further property on substantially the same trusts as those declared by the 1944 settlement for the benefit of Mr. Robert Macgowran Chapman's children. The third settlement, dated 10th February, 1950, was made on the occasion of the marriage of Henry James Nicholas Chapman (a son of Sir Robert and Lady Chapman) with Anne Barbara Croft. By it Lady Chapman settled property upon trusts for the children of that marriage, and upon similar trusts for the children of any subsequent marriage of Nicholas, and it was provided that in the event of the failure of these trusts the trustees should pay over the trust funds to the trustees of the settlement of 8th February, 1950, to be held on the trusts of that settlement.

Robert Macgowran Chapman was, at the date of the action, married to Barbara May Chapman, and there were three children of the marriage, born in 1941, 1944 and 1946. There were, at that time, no children of Nicholas's marriage.

In March 1952, the value of the funds comprised in the three settlements was approximately £78,000 and, because of the discretionary trusts for the common maintenance of Mr. Robert Chapman's children, contained in Clause 3 of the 1944 settlement and Clause 4 of the settlement of 8th February, 1950, the trustees of the settlements were advised that a claim for estate duty would arise in respect of the funds comprised in the 1944 settlement (amounting to £43,300) on the death of the survivor of Sir Robert Chapman (then aged 72) and of Lady Chapman (then aged 65) and in respect of the funds comprised in the 8th February, 1950 settlement upon the death of Lady Chapman. The trustees of the third settlement were also advised that if the substituted limitation contained in that settlement was valid and became effective, a claim for estate duty would arise in respect of their fund also. The total amount of estate duty involved would amount to nearly £30,000.

In these circumstances a scheme of arrangement was prepared with the object of avoiding these anticipated claims. This could only be effective if the first two settlements were freed from the provisions for common maintenance contained in clause 3 of the first, and clause 4 of the second, and it was therefore proposed that the trustees should, with the sanction of the Court, advance their funds to the trustees of a new settlement containing similar trusts, but with these clauses omitted. It was also proposed that the trustees of the third settlement should, on the failure of the trusts therein contained, similarly transfer their funds to the trustees of the new settlement.

This scheme, therefore, which required the consent of the Court to release the interests of the infant children of Mr. Robert Macgowran Chapman and also possible unborn children of Robert and Nicholas, who might at some future time have been beneficiaries under the settlements, was brought before Harman, J., in chambers, by way of originating summons on 28th July, 1952, and Harman, J., refused to sanction it, on the ground that he had no jurisdiction to do so, either under the inherent jurisdiction of the Court, or under Sect. 57 of the Trustee Act, 1925. The trustees appealed.

A majority of the Court of Appeal, Evershed, M.R., and Romer, L.J., upheld the decision of Harman, J. They took the view that there was no authority to sanction the scheme under Sect. 57 which, in their view, only empowers the Court to make orders with reference to the management or administration by trustees of the trust property. The scheme proposed in this case did not arise out of any administrative or managerial difficulty affecting the trust assets. It was really a scheme for rewriting the trust interests to avoid death duties.

It was, however, strongly pressed on behalf of the trustees that the Court had an unlimited jurisdiction in relation to the property of infants and unborn beneficiaries, which it would exercise whenever a suitable case for intervention is placed before it. This contention is summarised by Evershed, M.R., as follows—

> It was the argument of counsel for all the appellants (founded on Jeffrey, L.C.'s, case, *Earl of Winchelsea* v. *Norcliffe* and other early cases, including *Pierson* v. *Shore* before Hardwicke, L.C., and *Inwood* v. *Twyne* before Northington, L.C.) that the jurisdiction of the Court to modify or vary trusts and to direct the trustees accordingly was unlimited provided: (1) that all persons interested who were *sui juris* assented, and (2) that it was clearly shown to be for the advantage or convenience of all persons interested who were not *sui juris*, including persons unborn or not presently ascertainable; in other words, that the Court has unlimited jurisdiction in relation to the property of infants, including the beneficial interests of infants and unborn *cestuis que trust* under a settlement, and will exercise that jurisdiction so as to secure any benefit or advantage for the infants or unborn persons which they could have themselves secured had they been *in esse* and *sui juris*, even to the extent of sanctioning a departure from the beneficial trusts of the trust instrument from which the interests in question are derived.

The majority of the Court of Appeal were unable to agree that the inherent jurisdiction went so far. In particular, Lord

Evershed thought that the decisions in *Re New* and *Re Tollemache*, which have been discussed elsewhere, were against it. To the principle that the Court's jurisdiction does not extend to the remoulding of beneficial interests he thought that there were only two exceptions: (1) Trusts where a settlor has provided that the immediate beneficiaries have the fund for their present maintenance. In such cases the Court will assume an intention to provide[1]; and (2) cases where there is a genuine compromise between beneficiaries in respect of their rights under a settlement. Here the Court will approve the compromise on behalf of infants and unborn persons. The best-known illustration of the exercise of this jurisdiction is *Re Trenchard.* A rearrangement of interests to avoid a liability to estate duty which would otherwise exist is not, however, a compromise, but a substitution of new beneficial interests for those which existed before.

From this view, Denning, L.J., dissented. He thought that the early cases, from the time of Lord Chancellor Jeffreys onwards, showed that the Court did possess such an inherent jurisdiction, which it exercised in the interests of infants. In his view, therefore, cases in which maintenance had been authorised, where there was no provision for maintenance in the will or settlement, and cases in which the Court had sanctioned compromises on behalf of infants and unborn persons were simply specific illustrations of the exercise of a general jurisdiction. He also added that whenever the Court has, of its own motion, placed limitations on its own jurisdiction, *e.g.* in respect of lifting restraints on anticipation,[2] or in respect of the sale of heirlooms,[3] or in respect of the power of trustees to concur in the reconstruction or amalgamation of companies in which they held shares,[4] the legislature has been ready to intervene to remove these self-imposed limitations.[5] Finally he added—

> I would therefore myself allow the appeal in all these cases; and I am the more ready to do so because I am told that the

[1] *Havelock* v. *Havelock; Re Collins; Re Walker.* [2] *Robinson* v. *Wheelwright.*
[3] *D'Eyncourt* v. *Gregory.* [4] *Re New; Re Tollemache.*
[5] Conveyancing Act, 1881, Sect. 39: Law of Property Act, 1925, Sect. 169 (married women); Settled Land Act, 1925, Sect. 67 (heirlooms); Trustee Act, 1925, Sect. 10 (3) and Sect. 57 (shares).

Chancery judges in chambers have in the past exercised their jurisdiction in similar cases in a very beneficent manner and this is confirmed by the approval given to the schemes in *Re Salting*, by Eve, J., and in *Re Mair*, by Farwell, J., and in an unreported decision of Simonds, J., in 1938 under the inherent jurisdiction which was drawn to our attention. The jurisdiction has been so freely exercised that the rejection of the schemes in the present cases has taken Lincoln's Inn by surprise, so much so that many proposed schemes have been held up pending our decision. The practice of the profession in these cases is the best evidence of what the law is; indeed, it makes law. It would be most disturbing if we were to say that the Chancery judges for many years have been acting without jurisdiction. What would be the result? I suppose that the schemes could be ignored by the Revenue and by all persons not *sui juris*, which would be a very unsatisfactory state of affairs. It is not right to unsettle the jurisdiction of the Court on these matters unless some high principle demands it, and I see none.

By a majority, therefore, the appeal in the *Chapman* case failed. The *Downshire* appeal, however, raised different questions. Once again there was a proposal that interests under a settlement (one of them being the protected life interest of the Marquess of Downshire) should be exchanged for various other interests which would arise under the rewritten settlement. In this case, however, the property was settled under the Settled Land Act, 1925, and although Roxburgh, J., held in chambers that he had no jurisdiction, either under the inherent jurisdiction of the Court or under Sect. 64 of the Settled Land Act, 1925, the Court of Appeal took a different view. The Court agreed that this transaction could not be affected by the inherent jurisdiction of the Court, but they were prepared to regard the scheme in this case as a genuine compromise, and so was within the terms of Sect. 64, and he added—

The jurisdiction under Sect. 64 of the Settled Land Act, 1925, is, in our judgment, in some respects more ample in regard to the subject matter to which it relates than is Sect. 57 of the Trustee Act, 1925. If this result is regarded as unexpected, we point out that the language of the two sections is to a material degree dissimilar, and the conclusions which we have formed are based on what we regard, in each case, as the material meaning of the words used.

In the *Downshire* appeal, therefore, the Court accepted jurisdiction under Sect. 64, and sanctioned the reframed settlement as a compromise of interests.

The *Blackwell* appeal arose out of a voluntary settlement, made in 1933, by which the plaintiff settled a trust fund or protective trusts on himself for life, with remainder to his children and issue, as he should appoint, and in default of appointment, for his children in unequal shares, with an ultimate trust for his testamentary appointees. The plaintiff had one son, born in 1951. The value of the settled fund was £83,000 on which, on the plaintiff's death, estate duty would be payable at 65 per cent. The plaintiff asked the Court to sanction a scheme whereby he surrendered his life interest in half the settled fund, so as to accelerate the interests in remainder, upon terms that his life interest in the other half of the fund was not thereby forfeited. Once again Roxburgh, J., had held that there was no jurisdiction to sanction such a scheme, but once again the Court of Appeal took the view that, although Sect. 57 of the Trustee Act, 1925, was not wide enough to cover it, the scheme was essentially a compromise, similar in essentials to that in *Re Downshire*, although in this case, it was referred back to the judge with liberty to the parties to amend the scheme and make it more appropriate for the Court to sanction it under its inherent jurisdiction.

It will be apparent that in these three appeals, the majority of the Court felt that it had gone as far as it could towards sanctioning these schemes. One was approved under Sect. 64 of the Settled Land Act, 1925, one would be ultimately approved as a compromise under the Court's inherent jurisdiction, and the *Chapman* scheme only failed because it could not be regarded as a compromise, so that it could not be approved under the Court's inherent jurisdiction, and it was too wide to qualify for approval under Sect. 57 of the Trustee Act, 1925. The House of Lords, however, was less responsive to the desires of trustees and other interested parties. Since only the *Chapman* scheme had been rejected by the Court of Appeal, there was a further appeal to the House of Lords in this case only, and the House of Lords unanimously upheld the decision of the majority of the Court of Appeal. The principal ground upon which the majority of the members of the House of Lords based their view was that, although the Court undoubtedly had power to sanction compromises on behalf of infant beneficiaries, the scheme in *Chapman* v. *Chapman* could not properly be regarded as a compromise, since there was no real dispute between any of the beneficiaries as to the extent of their rights. What was sought to be done was, by way of bargain, to rearrange the beneficial interests. This, however, failed to solve the conundrum propounded by Lord Cohen who, although he did not dissent, expressed certain reservations concerning the conclusions reached by other members of the House in the following terms—

> My Lords, I am not satisfied that the Court, in sanctioning a compromise in the strict sense, is not exercising a jurisdiction to alter beneficial rights. It is true that in such a case the right has not been defined, but the right of the beneficiary is a right to that to which, upon its true construction, the will or settlement entitles him. The very essence of a compromise is that it may give each party something other than that which the will or settlement would, on its true construction, confer on them.

Lord Cohen also disposed of the problem concerning the validity of earlier exercises of the jurisdiction raised by Denning, L.J., in the passage from his judgment which has already been quoted. Lord Cohen said—

> I cannot sit down without expressing my doubt whether there is any foundation for the suggestion made by Denning, L.J., that the effect of your Lordships' decision may be that schemes sanctioned in the past could be ignored by the Revenue and by all persons not *sui juris*. The High Court is a superior court and the control of trustees is a matter within its jurisdiction. It would take a great deal of argument to satisfy me that its orders were a nullity and that trustees were not fully protected by orders made by that Court in the exercise of that trust jurisdiction even though your Lordships may, in a later case, have said the jurisdiction had been wrongly exercised.

Happily, no Court has been subsequently called upon to consider an argument upon the effect of an order made by a superior court, either in excess of, or without jurisdiction to make it.

Behind the technical arguments upon the question whether the earlier decisions were simply illustrations of the exercise of a general inherent jurisdiction or whether they were to be regarded simply as specific cases in which a Court would act was the broader question of the use of this jurisdiction to mitigate the rigours of modern taxation. This point was dealt with by Lord Morton of Henryton at the conclusion of his speech, where he observes—

> If the Court had power to approve, and did approve, schemes such as the present scheme, the way would be open for a most undignified game of chess between the Chancery Division and the legislature. The alteration of one settlement for the purposes of avoiding taxation already imposed might well be followed by scores of successful applications for a similar purpose by beneficiaries under other settlements. The legislature might then counter this move by imposing fresh taxation upon the settlements as thus altered. The beneficiaries would then troop back to the Chancery Division and say: "Please alter the trusts again. You have the power, the adults desire it, and it is for the benefit of the infants to avoid this fresh taxation. The legislature may not move again!" So the game might go on, if the judges of the Chancery Division had the power which the appellants claim for them, and if they thought it right to make the first move.

Since, however, the Court of Appeal took the view that the *Blackwell* and *Downshire* schemes were compromises, this is presumably the situation which now exists in respect of settlements of this type. In *Re Simmons* Danckwerts, J., held that Sect. 64 of the Settled Land Act, 1925, permitted him to authorise the trustees of a trust for sale of land to assent to a scheme whereby the tenant for life obtained a larger capital sum in lieu of certain other interests, on the ground that the powers conferred by Sect. 64 were exercisable by trustees for sale by virtue of Sect. 28 (1) of the Law of Property Act, 1925.

It can scarcely be questioned, however, that the decision of the House of Lords in *Chapman* v. *Chapman*, taken in conjunction with the decisions of the Court of Appeal in the *Blackwell* and *Downshire* appeals left the law in an uncertain and unsatisfactory state, and accordingly the question of the extent of the Court's jurisdiction in these cases was in March, 1957, referred to the Law Reform Committee.

The report of the Committee, which appeared in the following November,[1] proved to be a striking vindication of the views expressed in the Court of Appeal by Lord Justice Denning, and in particular of his observation that whenever the Court has voluntarily restricted the exercise of its jurisdiction, the legislature has subsequently conferred the power, the existence of which has been doubted. The Committee were unanimously of opinion that the distinctions which have followed *Chapman* v. *Chapman*, depending as they did upon the constructions given to Sect. 57 of the Trustee Act, 1925, and to Sect. 64 of the Settled Land Act, 1925, were indefensible and irrelevant, and they thought that it should be made clear that the position should be restored to that which it had been generally thought to be in *Chapman* v. *Chapman*. Moreover, the Committee completely rejected the fears expressed by Lord Morton, which have already been mentioned. The fact that tax avoidance schemes were sometimes of a questionable character was no justification for rejecting schemes where the rearrangement of beneficial interests was not open to objection, and which would give rise to no possible criticism, were it not for the fact that sanction in respect of the beneficial interests of infants or lunatics was required. Perhaps the most striking feature of the report is the frank recognition which it gives to the fact that changing social circumstances have rendered inevitable intervention by the Court of the type which, prior to *Chapman* v. *Chapman* had been regarded as a normal exercise of jurisdiction. There is, in fact, no sound reason why a scheme which would otherwise give rise to no legal difficulty, should become impracticable simply because it requires the consent of the Court on behalf of an unborn, infant, or lunatic beneficiary. Such a limitation of jurisdiction adversely affects, not only the person under a disability himself (whose welfare should be the Court's primary concern) but also all others with interests under the settlement, who are subject to no disability.[2]

[1] Cmnd. 310.

[2] The Variation of Trusts Act, 1958, which was introduced as a private bill and which embodies the proposals of the Law Reform Committee, received the Royal Assent on 23rd July, 1958.

CHAPTER VI

The Director as Trustee

The extent to which a director of a commercial company can be regarded as a trustee is an interesting inquiry for three principal reasons: (1) it is the point at which commercial practice touches equity practice, and the two jurisdictions might be expected to have widely differing outlooks upon major problems; (2) the conception of the director as a trustee is a modern one, having been developed mainly since the passing of the first Companies Acts in the middle of the nineteenth century; and (3) the differing outlooks of the Courts of Common Law and the Court of Chancery upon the position of the director was one of the reasons leading to the fusion of the administration of Law and Equity by the Judicature Acts, 1873–1875.[1]

It is probably due to the first reason that the extent to which the ordinary obligations of a trustee prevail against a director is a matter of some uncertainty, and that the attitude of the courts has fluctuated considerably in the course of a century. The old joint stock company, created either by statute or royal charter, had undergone very considerable development in the eighteenth century. By two Acts of 1834 and 1837 the Crown was empowered, in suitable cases, to restrict the liability of members even of unincorporated trading companies to a fixed maximum for each share. Such a privilege could only be enjoyed where a registered deed of partnership existed, in which the capital was divided into specific shares. The necessity for the registration of the deed of partnership was the beginning of the Register of Joint Stock Companies, and from this point the transition to the modern

[1] Holdsworth, *History of English Law*, Vol. 1, p. 638.

limited liability company was continuous. In 1844 and 1845, six statutes dealt with various types of company, and for the first time the limited company, with its Memorandum and Articles of Association, emerges. So also do many of the most characteristic features of modern company practice, including the appointment of directors, the general and extraordinary meetings of shareholders, and the preparation and audit of an annual balance sheet. Finally, two statutes passed in 1855 and 1856 introduced the great principle that any group of persons engaging in trade or commerce (other than insurance and banking) could be incorporated with limited liability on satisfying certain specified requirements. In 1862 the first consolidating statute was passed.

If the provisions of these successive Acts are considered, it will be found that, whilst the legislature was carefully exploring the possibilities of such a potent instrument for industrial development as the limited liability company undoubtedly was, it was also seeking to preserve, as far as possible in the changed circumstances, some of the main features of the older joint stock company. The Court of Chancery had a similar outlook. For example, the third edition of John William Smith's *Mercantile Law* was published in 1866, and the reader of that treatise will find that, even at that date, the learned author devotes no less than forty pages to joint stock companies, under which he discusses both the older joint stock company proper, and the later statutory creation. The author obviously regards the principles governing the former as applicable, *mutatis mutandis*, to statutory companies. That being so, his observations on the duties of directors of joint stock companies are of especial interest. He says—

> As the management of the company is confided by the deed of settlement to the directors and their agents, and the bulk of the shareholders must necessarily continue passive, the courts of equity are very strict in enforcing the due execution of the trust reposed in those functionaries. In *Wallworth* v. *Holt*, the affairs of a joint stock bank having fallen into a very disastrous condition, the Lord Chancellor entertained a bill against the public officer, directors and trustees, filed by some of the shareholders on behalf of the rest, praying for an account of the assets, and a due application of them to the liabilities. The

> authority of this case has been recognised, and the rule laid down by it acted upon in several recent instances, in some of which an attempt has also been made to extend the relief to a decree for the dissolution of the company, but the courts have refused to entertain a bill for such a purpose, without making the whole of the members parties to the suit. Where a projected company has never been brought into actual operation, the persons who have advanced money on the faith of the completion of the undertaking may maintain an action to recover it. And equity will give effectual relief where a scheme turns out a mere bubble, concocted in fraud.

In this extract, Smith bases his observations upon the fact that in the company formed by deed of settlement, the directors were trustees in the full sense, the firm's property being vested in them in that capacity. At first, it was assumed that the directors of a statutory company were in a similar position.

Unfortunately, the promise of these earlier decisions was not fulfilled, and the late Professor Jenks, in his lively *Short History of English Law* commenting on the failure of equity in the nineteenth century to remedy new abuses, wrote—

> The second example is that of the company promoter or director, who shields himself from liability towards his real beneficiaries, the shareholders, behind the artificial protection of that purely legal entity, the company. With a reasonable application of equitable principles, the monstrous doctrine: that "the directors of a company are not trustees for individual shareholders", would never have been adopted; and directors who are secretly negotiating a profitable sale of their company's assets would not be allowed to go about buying up shares with a view to profiting at the expense of their own shareholders. The Court which decided *Keech* v. *Sandford* would have made short work of such a claim.

These observations were patently written with the well-known case of *Percival* v. *Wright*[2] freshly in the author's mind. In that case the facts were very much as summarised in Professor Jenks's observations, and the Court of Appeal showed great tenderness in protecting the chairman of the company, who had purchased the holdings of some of the shareholders. Swinfen Eady, J., flatly rejected the suggestion that the direc-

[1] *Mercantile Law*, 3rd Ed. (1866), pp. 131–2.

[2] It is, of course, possible that the company itself might have recovered a profit made by directors as a result of the misuse of confidential information.

tors could be held to be trustees for individual shareholders, and was at considerable pains to show how difficult it would be if directors were compelled to disclose pending negotiations. It might perhaps have been thought that one way to avoid embarrassment would be for directors to refrain from buying shareholders' interests when they were on the eve of concluding a profitable arrangement for the company. Perhaps they might even have suggested to shareholders that they should hold on to their shares a little longer. Such a way out does not appear to have suggested itself to the learned judge, however, and he contented himself with saying—

> The sound rule appears to be that shareholders must be taken to know, and are fixed with knowledge of, the powers conferred by the constitution of the company upon the directors, and there is no more reason for the shareholders to assume that the directors were not negotiating for a sale of the property, if they have a power of sale, than to assume, if not stated, that they were not exercising any other powers conferred upon them by the constitution of the company.

If we substitute for "director," the word "trustee," and for "shareholder" the term "*cestui que trust*" the contrast is startling. Demonstrably a different social outlook has prevailed in the case of directors, as compared with that applicable to trustees. Nevertheless, if we turn to one of the early decisions on the responsibility of directors, *Aberdeen Railway Company* v. *Blakie Brothers*, we find Lord Cranworth, L.C., saying—

> A corporate body can only act by agents, and it is of course the duty of those agents so to act as best to promote the interests of the corporation whose affairs they are conducting. Such agents have duties to discharge of a fiduciary nature towards their principal. And it is a rule of universal application, that no one, having such duties to discharge, shall be allowed to enter into engagements in which he has, or can have, a personal interest conflicting or which possibly may conflict, with the interests of those whom he is bound to protect. So strictly is this principle adhered to, that no question is allowed to be raised as to the fairness or unfairness of a contract entered into.

Evidently by the end of the century this principle, which is in the direct line of descent from the equitable principles enunciated by Lord Hardwicke in *The Earl of Chesterfield* v. *Janssen*, has been confined within narrow limits. Something will be said shortly of the reason for this miscarriage of equity. The principle, indeed, owes its origin to Lord Hardwicke, for in *Charitable Corporation* v. *Sutton*, decided in 1742, he had held that committeemen (that is to say, directors) of a chartered corporation, who had misapplied its funds and broken its by-laws were liable on the footing of trustees for breach of trust. Such committeemen under the deed of settlement would have the property vested in them as trustees in the full sense. It is also significant that in *York and North Midland Railway* v. *Hudson*, a case decided the year before *Aberdeen Railway Company* v. *Blakie Brothers* reached the House of Lords, Romilly, M.R., had held directors who had wrongly applied the funds of a company liable on the footing of trustees. The facts of this case are exceedingly interesting. Hudson was the chairman and the dominating influence in the railway company. His efforts were largely responsible for an extension of the company's running powers. To finance developments, additional capital was called for, and Hudson induced the shareholders at a general meeting to place a large number of shares "at the disposal of the directors." That was, in fact, equivalent to placing them at his own disposal, and he placed them on the register in the name of a nominee, subsequently reselling them at a profit. The Master of the Rolls ordered an account of the proceeds of the sales of these shares, observing—

> The directors are persons selected to manage the affairs of the company for the benefit of the shareholders. It is an office of trust, which, if they undertake, it is their duty to perform fully and entirely. A resolution by the shareholders, therefore, that shares or any other species of property should be at the disposal of the directors, is a resolution that it shall be at the disposal of the trustees, in other words, that the persons entrusted with that property shall dispose of it within the scope of the functions delegated to them in the manner best suited to benefit their *cestuis que trust*. To construe these words as importing a gift to the directors for their individual advantage, or as investing them with a secret and irresponsible trust, would, in my opinion, be impossible unless they were coupled with clear and unambiguous expressions to that effect.

In the absence of any such expressions, not only the obligation of discharging the duty lies upon persons accepting the trust, but also the further obligation of accounting for their discharge of it to their *cestuis que trust* whenever required.

In *Hudson's* case it was the company which proceeded against the director, and towards the company the director can be regarded as a trustee, to be proceeded against on that footing. Thus, *Hudson's* case is an illustration of the observations of Lord Cranworth in *Aberdeen Railway Company* v. *Blakie Brothers.* For the same reason, it was held that directors, being trustees, could not claim the benefit of the Statutes of Limitation, *even though they were also agents of the company*, before the passing of the Trustee Act, 1888.[1] Such a position is effective where there are officials or directors willing and able to proceed against defaulting directors. Where these do not exist, the narrowness of the protection, due to the exclusion of shareholders from the status of *cestuis que trust* becomes apparent.

It is certainly the case that before the passing of the nineteenth-century Companies Acts, the directors of joint stock companies had been regarded as trustees in the wider sense. Indeed, such a situation was inevitable, for before the Acts of 1844–5, joint stock companies were not incorporated, unless a statute or royal charter conferred this privilege. Accordingly, the strict antithesis between "trustee for the company" and "trustee for the shareholders" which appears in the later decisions could not arise. However, there exists one important distinction between a trustee in the ordinary sense and a director of a modern limited liability company. The trustee was the owner of the trust property. A director of a statutory company does not have the ownership of the company's property vested in him as his predecessor under a deed of settlement did. Such a situation is not necessarily fatal to the existence of fiduciary obligations, as the relationship of solicitor and client shows. Still, it does emphasise that from the standpoint of the common law courts, the status of the director was that of agent for the company, and an agent's responsibilities are not necessarily those of a trustee. Historically, this

[1] *Flitcroft's* case.

seems to have been the starting point of the modern tendency to reduce progressively the responsibilities of the director. The Court of Chancery started by exacting high standards from him. Under the influence of the common law courts they relaxed their standards, and eventually they went to extreme lengths to relieve the director from responsibility, at any rate towards his shareholders. In this instance, the Judicature Acts appear to have operated in reverse. Equitable principles gave way to those applied at common law.

If the very numerous decisions on the position of directors given between 1860 and 1885 are examined, the difficulties of these differing attitudes of the two jurisdictions are manifest. So also are the efforts made to resolve them. These can be traced in large measure to the judgment of Lord Cairns (whilst Lord Justice of Appeal) in *Ferguson* v. *Wilson* where he points out that where shareholders are proceeding against directors for misapplication of the company's assets, then the directors are in the position of trustees and can be proceeded against on that footing. This was repeatedly reaffirmed, more especially by Jessel, M.R., in *Re Forest of Dean Company*, and by that great master of company law, Lord Lindley, in 1894, when still a member of the Court of Appeal, in *Re Lands Allotment Co.*, where he says—

> Although directors are not, properly speaking, trustees, yet they have always been considered and treated as trustees of moneys which come to their hands, or which is actually under their control, and ever since joint stock companies were invented directors have been held liable to make good moneys which they have misapplied, upon the same footing as if they were trustees.

Thus, the assets are regarded as a trust fund, which, if misapplied, can be followed into the hands of any one taking with knowledge of the misapplication.

Where directors act on behalf of the company, however, they must be regarded as agents. In such cases, as Lord Cairns pointed out in *Ferguson* v. *Wilson*, "they are merely agents of the company. The company itself cannot act in its own person, for it has no person, it can only act through directors, and the case is, as regards those directors, merely the ordinary case of principal and agent, for wherever an agent is liable those directors would be liable. Where the liability would attach to the principal, and the principal only, the liability is the liability of the company."

Even in agency cases, however, there may be a fiduciary relationship between the director and the company. Equity has merely acquiesced in the exclusion of a further duty towards the shareholders individually—a situation which, in reality, is a logical inference from the fact of incorporation. The extent of the responsibility of the director to the company is clearly brought out in two cases which are reported consecutively in the reports—*Cooks* v. *Deeks* and *Jacobus Marler Estates* v. *Marler*. In the former, the Privy Council compelled the directors of a Canadian company to restore to the company the benefits of contracts made by them personally, by diverting contracts formerly enjoyed by the company, and it further affirmed that the transactions could not stand even though a shareholders' resolution had ratified the contracts, inasmuch as the directors controlled a majority of the votes. This is an illustration of the general principle that in equity an agent cannot, without the consent of his principal, given with full knowledge of the material facts and without undue influence on the part of the agent, retain any profit from a transaction entered into by him as agent.

It will be evident, therefore, that in handling the assets of a company, directors are accountable on the footing of trustees strictly, in cases of active misapplication (for example, for purposes not permitted by the memorandum of association). In respect of contracts entered into by them in respect of the company's business, they are regarded as agents standing in a fiduciary position to the company. Where, however, the courts have failed to apply the trust concept to directors is (1) in respect of individual shareholders, as was apparent from the decision in *Percival* v. *Wright*; and (2) in respect of the degree of care and business prudence expected from directors in the discharge of their duties. It was here that the failure to apply normal equitable standards was most apparent, as will be evident from one or two illustrations which will be discussed shortly. One may speculate on the reasons for this striking attitude. A Marxist might say that it was due to the entry of the upper classes into commerce through the convenient device of limited liability. A less biased sociologist might suggest that it was due to the anxiety of the courts not unduly to hamper business men in their normal pursuits. However that might be, the results were sometimes startling. One further point which may perhaps be made is that, however low might be the standards prescribed by the Court, those prescribed by commercial practice were substantially lower. The law did at least prescribe *some* standard of care for the company director. The articles of particular companies frequently attempted to relieve him completely of responsibility for what he did. No doubt this had something to do with the attitude of the courts. It would have been somewhat ludicrous, or even hypocritical, for courts to lay down strict standards of duty for directors, when company articles regularly allowed them to evade any standards prescribed by the Court.

One other circumstance forcibly presents itself to those who examine the attitude of the courts towards directors. Judges were evidently impressed by the fact that a directorship was a very part-time occupation. A business man is a busy man, and if he is, in addition, the director of several companies, then the amount of time he can devote to the affairs of any single company is of necessity very limited. Conversely, if the director is of the guinea-pig variety—if, for example, he is a distinguished nobleman with wide social and sporting activities—then his attention to business may be fleeting, and his abilities limited. Accordingly (the decisions suggest) he is not to be victimised, if the consequences of his somewhat fugitive appearances in the board-room are not always happy. Once again the contrast between this attitude and that of a court of equity towards a trustee in the strict sense is striking.

It is to be regretted that a full-scale sociological inquiry into the working of our company law during the hundred years of its existence has not yet been undertaken. Various writers, however, have at different times touched upon particular aspects of this wide subject. Thus, Mr. H. B. Samuel in *Shareholders' Money*, written nearly twenty years ago, shortly after the *Kylsant* case, devoted an important part of his highly-interesting book to an analysis of some of the best-known decisions on the liability of company directors in their social background, from which some interesting facts emerged. Thus, by analysing the 1932 edition of the *Directory of Directors*, he found that a total of 654 English peers held between them 562 directorates. Marquises, oddly enough, were the most popular, since for a total of twenty-five marquises there were thirty directorates. These figures completely excluded from consideration any peers who inherited directorates in family businesses, as well as peers who actually worked in City firms. The consequence of appointing to boards persons of eminence, whose acquaintance with the affairs of the company was slight, was sometimes disastrous.

Actions by shareholders against directors for mismanagement have usually included allegations that the directors have been guilty either of fraud, negligence, or misfeasance. Fraud, as is well known, was the substance of the action in *Derry* v. *Peek*. It was in consequence of the decision of the House of Lords in this case that the Directors' Liability Act, 1890, was passed, and the provisions of that Act, imposing a special statutory responsibility for statements in a company prospectus, were incorporated into later Companies Acts. It is no part of the purpose of this lecture to analyse the definition of fraud given by the House of Lords in this case. What is of direct relevance, however, is the fact that the members of the House of Lords on that occasion showed no disposition to apply the principles of fraud as developed by courts of equity in respect of fiduciary relationships to the office of company director. Having absolved the directors of the Plymouth, Devonport and District Tramways from the stigma of common law fraud in this case, they regarded their task as complete. Indeed, Lord Herschell, in his speech, expressly stated that actions for abuse of fiduciary relationships had no application to cases of the kind before the Court.

There is, however, one further aspect of *Derry* v. *Peek* which is not without interest in the present discussion. Lord Bramwell noticed that the directors of the tramway company had received their directors' shares from the promoter, who was intending to sell the enterprise to the company. Commenting on this, Lord Bramwell said—

> It is wonderful to me that honest men of ordinary intelligence cannot see the impropriety of this. It is obvious that the contractor can only give this qualification because he means to get it back in the price given for the work he is to do. That price is to be fixed by the directors who have taken his money. They are paid by him to give him a good price, as high a price as they can, while their duty to the shareholders is to give him one as low as they can. But there is another thing. The public, seeing these names, might well say, "They are respectable and intelligent men who think well enough of this scheme to adventure their money in it; we will do the same," little knowing that those thus trusted had made themselves safe against loss if the thing turned out ill, while they might gain if it was successful.

Plain hints of this kind, however, were unheeded. The supply of guinea-pigs was apparently inexhaustible. It is only necessary to consider from this standpoint *Re Cardiff Savings Bank: The Marquis of Bute's* case, remembering Mr. Samuel's observations on the ratio of marquises to directorships. The Cardiff Savings Bank was formed in 1819, and was reconstituted under the Trustee Savings Bank Act, 1863, in that year. It suspended payment with heavy liabilities in 1886, and a liquidator was appointed. The subsequent proceedings showed that loss had resulted from the irregular conduct of the bank's business by its trustees and managers. The question in the present case was whether the Marquis of Bute shared responsibility for the loss resulting from the irregularities. The marquis was the (unpaid) president of the bank, and it was shown that he had attended no meetings of its governing body for seventeen years. Nevertheless, it was held that he had committed no actionable breach of duty. Stirling, J., in this case preferred to minimise the marquis's functions as trustee, and said that the standard of care to be shown by him could not be placed higher than that of a company director who, he added, must exercise care at the meetings at which he was actually present, but who owed no duty to attend any specific meeting, or even any company meeting at all! This "intermittent" theory of a director's duties has frequently been approved in later cases. How far it might be pressed was indicated in the concluding remarks of Stirling, J., in his judgment in *The Marquis of Bute's* case—

> To hold that the marquis was guilty of neglect or omission in respect of this duty, in the absence of any knowledge or notice that it was not duly performed, would, in my opinion, be to fix him with liability for the neglect and omission of others rather than his own. It was much pressed on me that, if this be so, all the trustees and managers might abstain from acting, leaving the business to be transacted by the officers of the bank alone, and yet escape liability. I have difficulty in seeing how this could happen without the knowledge of some at least of the trustees and managers. However this may be, it is not the present case. The affairs of the bank were, in fact, managed by some of the trustees and managers; and I do not think it necessary to inquire how matters would have stood if no trustee or manager had taken part in the conduct of the business.

Two interesting conclusions can be drawn from these remarks—

(1) A manager and trustee who continuously absents himself from meetings is in a safer legal position than one who attends, either regularly or intermittently.

(2) So long as one manager and trustee supervised the bank officials, apparently none of the absentees could be made liable for what he did or failed to do. It should be added that the savings bank was not incorporated, although the marquis appears to have been considered as if he were director. Evidently lax company practice was influencing the law of trusts.

The soundness of Stirling, J.'s, estimate of the director's degree of responsibility was shown by the opinions of members of the House of Lords in *Dovey* v. *Cory*. This was an action by the liquidator against Mr. Cory for misfeasance as a company director, on the failure of the National Bank of Wales. The bank was alleged to have paid dividends out of capital[1] and although the directors stated every year in their report that provision was made for bad debts, this was in fact not

[1] The Court of Appeal doubted whether they had done this, and the House of Lords did not overrule the Court of Appeal.

done. The true state of affairs was known only to the managing director. Cory was a director who could have discovered the true position by analysing the weekly and quarterly statements issued to directors. Moreover, he was present at two meetings of the board when minutes were read mentioning the receipt of letters from the company's auditors. He failed to ask what the letters were about, and, if he had done, he would have discovered that the auditors were stressing the necessity of forthwith making provision for bad debts. The House of Lords held that Cory had not been guilty of negligence in his duties as a director. It was certainly clear that Cory was not at any time privy to the fraudulent way in which the company's business was being transacted. The House of Lords unanimously held that he had not been negligent either. Lord Davey put the whole matter in a nutshell when he said—

> I think the respondent was bound to give his attention to and exercise his judgment as a man of business on the matters which were brought before the board at the meetings which he attended, and it is not proved that he did not do so. But I think he was entitled to rely upon the judgment, information, and advice of the chairman and general manager, as to whose integrity, skill and competence he had no reason for suspicion. . . . It was the duty of the general manager and (possibly) the chairman to go carefully through the returns from the branches, and to bring before the board any matter requiring their consideration, but the respondent was not, in my opinion, guilty of negligence in not examining them for himself, notwithstanding that they were laid on the table of the board for reference.

It is difficult to conceive of greater tenderness for the director than this. It evokes no responsive echo in the decisions of most jurisdictions in the United States. Unhappily, this well-known tenderness has coincided, in the past, with a succession of cases in which the incapacity or non-attendance of ornamental directors has enabled mismanagement or worse to remain undetected for long periods. How far this could go is well illustrated by *Re Brazilian Rubber Plantations and Estates, Limited.* The firm of C. W. & E. Meiter secured an option on rubber estates in Brazil for a purchase price of £15,000. After the property had passed through several hands, each time at a large profit, it was resold to a company formed for the purpose for £150,000. The company was in reality formed by the persons through whose hands the property had already passed at a substantial profit to themselves. The company's directors, however, were men of different status, and are described in the report as follows—

> The directors of the company, Sir Arthur Aylmer, Bart., Henry William Tugwell, Edward Barber, and Edward Henry Hancock, were all induced to become directors by Harbord or persons acting with him in the promotion of the company. Sir Arthur Aylmer was absolutely ignorant of business. He only consented to act because he was told the office would give a little pleasant employment without his incurring any responsibility.[1] H. W. Tugwell was partner in a firm of bankers in a good position in Bath; he was seventy-five years of age and very deaf; he was induced to join the board by representations made to him in January, 1906. Barber was a rubber broker and was told that all he would have to do would be to give an opinion as to the value of rubber when it arrived in England. Hancock was a man of business, who said he was induced to join by seeing the names of Tugwell and Barber, whom he considered good men.

So equipped, the new venture went forth, with grossly misleading statements in the prospectus, based on a report made by Meiter, who had first purchased the option, when the purchase price of the estates was £15,000. He had never been near the estates, and the report was written in London. The company duly purchased at £150,000, and it is scarcely surprising that it ran into heavy weather and swiftly sank. The liquidator sought to make the directors liable, but the Court held that the directors honestly believed the contract to be a beneficial one for the company, so that there was no misfeasance. In any event, even if the Court had held their omissions to be misfeasance, the indemnity clause would have fully protected them. Even so, it is valuable to consider the terms in which Neville, J., in this remarkable case, defined the director's obligations—

[1] The articles contained an indemnity clause in very wide terms.

It has been laid down that, so long as they act honestly, they cannot be made responsible in damages unless guilty of gross negligence. There is admittedly a want of precision in this statement of a director's liability. In truth, one cannot say whether a man has been guilty of negligence, gross or otherwise, unless one can determine what is the extent of the duty which he is alleged to have neglected. A director's duty has been laid down as requiring him to act with such care as is reasonably to be expected from him, having regard to his knowledge and experience. He is, I think, not bound to bring any special qualifications to his office. He may undertake the management of a rubber company in complete ignorance of everything connected with rubber, without incurring responsibility for the mistakes which may result from such ignorance; while if he is acquainted with the rubber business he must give the company the advantage of his knowledge when transacting the company's business. He is not, I think, bound to take any definite part in the conduct of the company's business; but, so far as he does undertake it, he must use reasonable care in its dispatch. Such reasonable care must, I think, be measured by the care an ordinary man might be expected to take in the same circumstances on his own behalf. He is clearly, I think, not responsible for damages occasioned by errors of judgment.

Following which observations one may reasonably inquire what a director *is* liable for.

Fourteen years later, in *Re City Equitable Fire Insurance Co.*, the Court of Appeal once again discussed the director's position, and their judgments form the last full exposition of the question, and the basis for the principles generally cited in textbooks. Once again, it should be noticed, the views of the Court did not affect the question of the directors' freedom from liability, for the usual indemnity clause again appeared in the articles, and the directors could shelter behind that. However, the case merits a fairly close analysis. Its essential facts are summarised in the opening paragraph of Romer, J.'s, judgment—

"On June 27, 1916, Gerard Lee Bevan became a director of the City Equitable Fire Insurance Co., Ltd. The company at that time was carrying on successfully the business of reinsurance of fire and marine risks, and was in a sound financial condition. On February 14, 1922, an order was made for the winding-up of the company by the Court. A searching investigation of the affairs of the company was then made, and this investigation disclosed a shortage in the funds of which the company should have been possessed by over £1,200,000. This deplorable state of affairs was in no way due to the company's trading operations as a reinsurance company. From the year 1916 onwards to February 28, 1921, which was the date of the company's last published balance sheet, there was a steady and most remarkable increase in the premium income of the company, due principally to the fact that it had been able to secure a large part of the business of the Munich Reinsurance Co., who before the outbreak of war had done most of the reinsurance business in this country. For the year ending February, 1916, the company's premium income for all classes of insurance was £363,000. For the year ending February, 1919, the premium income on fire and general account was £613,483, and on marine account was £1,351,000. For the year ending February, 1920, the corresponding figures were £1,189,759 and £1,422,471, and for the year ending February, 1921, they were £2,071,515 and £1,469,197. In each of the years 1919, 1920, and 1921 there was a large and progressive trading profit. The collapse of the company was not, therefore, due to its reinsurance business. It was entirely due to the following causes. Various industrial investments of the company, of which the net cost of the company had been £701,739, have realised, or are estimated to realise, £202,373, representing a loss of close upon £500,000. Over £445,000 of the company's funds had been applied in acquiring an interest in certain lands in Brazil, and this interest is estimated at the present time to be worth about £100,000 only. No less a sum than £110,000 had found its way into the hands of the company's manager in circumstances to be detailed hereafter, and none of that money is recoverable. A sum of £385,000 odd was due from Ellis & Co., the company's brokers, of which Bevan was the senior partner; and against this indebtedness the company held collateral security that has realised under £31,000. In respect of the balance it is estimated that only about £14,000 will ultimately be received as dividend in the bankruptcy of that firm. Bevan himself had misappropriated other moneys of the company amounting to nearly £7,000, and some £9,000 had been lent by Bevan or Ellis & Co. to a company, known as the Saskatoon Grain Co., without any authority whatever. Little, if anything, will be recovered in respect of these two sums. Nearly the whole of these enormous losses were brought about through Bevan's instrumentality, and a large part of them by his deliberate fraud. For that fraud he has been tried and convicted, and is now suffering the just penalty. But the question not unnaturally arises as to whether, during the period covered by Bevan's nefarious activities, the other directors and the auditors of the company were properly discharging the duties that they owed to the company's shareholders. The official receiver, as the liquidator of the company, alleges that they were not. He has accordingly included them, or such of them as are still living, as respondents, to the summons which he issued against Bevan . . . and whilst admitting, and rightly admitting, that they have acted honestly throughout, he claims that they have been guilty of such negligence as to render themselves liable in damages."

The judgment of Romer, J. (as he then was) in this case is a mine of information upon the duty owed by directors in discharging the affairs of the company. Whilst agreeing that a director stood in a fiduciary relationship to the company, he doubted whether the statement that the director was a trustee had much further significance. He further pointed out, what is indeed apparent, that his duty would also be affected by the size of the firm, the standing of its administrative officers, and the distribution of business between the board and the staff. This was, indeed, an elaboration of the remarks of Lord Macnaghten in *Dovey* v. *Cory*, in which he doubts whether precise rules for the conduct of company business can be formulated. The learned judge also agrees that in the discharge of his office, the director must exercise some degree of skill and diligence, although "to the question of what is the particular degree of skill and diligence required of him, the authorities do not give any very clear answer." The standard is certainly not very high. Indeed, the learned judge was in any event bound by the opinions of the House of Lords in *Overend, Gurney & Co.* v. *Gibb*, which are as follows—

> Whether or not the directors exceeded the powers entrusted to them, or whether if they did not so exceed their powers they were cognisant of circumstances of such a character, so plain, so manifest, and so simple of appreciation, that no men with any ordinary degree of prudence, acting on their own behalf, would have entered into such a transaction as they entered into.

Romer, J., adds these three other principles—

(1) A director need not exhibit in the performance of his duties a greater degree of skill than may reasonably be expected from a person of his knowledge and experience.

(2) A director is not bound to give continuous attention to the affairs of his company. His duties are of an intermittent nature to be performed at periodical board meetings, and at meetings of any committee of the board upon which he happens to be placed. He is not, however, bound to attend all such meetings, though he ought to attend whenever, in the circumstances, he is reasonably able to do so.

(3) In respect of all duties that, having regard to the exigencies of business and the articles of association, may properly be left to some other official, a director is, in the absence of grounds for suspicion, justified in trusting that official to perform such duties honestly.

Behind the careful enunciation of these principles there can be discerned the conception of the able and efficient man of business, interested perhaps in many companies, who can rapidly sum up the position of the company from reasonably regular attendance at board meetings. Nevertheless, these principles also permit boards of directors to include incompetents with high-sounding titles, who attend rarely if ever, and whose effective contribution to any directors' meeting may be difficult to detect. They may not even be aware of the manner in which the permanent officials of the company are conducting its business. It would seem not unreasonable to suggest, therefore, that the reported decisions show that the courts have been remarkably sympathetic to the not-so-competent director, and that the statement that the director has the responsibilities of a trustee is of very restricted significance when applied to the director's position. It is true that the Companies Act of 1948 took some steps towards making the responsibilities of directors in one or two matters more precise than they had been before,[1] but in this respect the Act of 1948 is in no sense revolutionary, and it is a matter for consideration whether, even today, it would not be advisable to define the duties of directors positively, especially in regard to the supervision of the general policy of the company whose affairs they direct. In one respect however, there has been an important improvement in the law since the *City Equitable Fire Insurance* case, in that the Act of 1929, and now Sect. 205 of the Act of 1948, makes void the indemnity clause which was common form in company articles before 1929, although, by Sect. 448, a director may obtain relief in cases of default if he has acted reasonably and honestly and ought fairly to be excused.

One final point may perhaps be noticed. The courts have not yet been called upon to determine the liability of members of boards of nationalised industries, but it may be hazarded that the standards applicable would be those of the directors of public companies. Whether this is an entirely satisfactory solution to the problem is also a matter for consideration.

[1] For example, in general, loans by a public company to a director are now prohibited: Sect. 190.

CHAPTER VII

The Charity Muddle

On 3rd November, 1913, Caleb Diplock made a will which contained a clause that the testator's executors should apply the whole of his residuary estate "for such charitable institution or institutions or other charitable or benevolent object or objects in England" as the executors thought fit. If the will had simply read that the executors should apply the whole of the residue "for such charitable institutions" as the executors should select, there would have been no problem, the legal profession would have been much poorer, and a number of charitable foundations, as well as the executors, would have been a good deal richer.

The testator died on 23rd March, 1936, and the executors (one of whom was a lawyer) assumed that the clause gave them power to distribute the residue (which amounted to about £263,000) to such charities as they should select. Accordingly, during the next three years, they distributed over £200,000 amongst 139 charities selected by them. During 1939, however, it occurred to some of the next of kin that the clause in the will might not give the executors the authority they had exercised, and in 1940 an action was brought by forty-eight next-of-kin, against the executors, the charities and the Attorney-General. This action reached the House of Lords in 1944, when their Lordships vindicated the earlier authorities by holding that the term "benevolent" is wider than the term "charitable", so that if executors are allowed to distribute between "charitable *or* benevolent" purposes, the parts to be distributed to each cannot be separated, and the whole gift is therefore void for uncertainty and lapses. In this case, as it was the residue which lapsed, the next-of-kin were entitled to it.[1]

So ended the first phase of this fascinating case, during which there had been some illuminating discussion of the possible meaning which the phrase "charitable or benevolent" might bear. For example, if I say that my profession is that of counsel, or barrister, I am equating the terms "counsel" and "barrister," and "or" is there used with the sense of "*id est*." This, however, is not the normal meaning of "or," and it was not its meaning in *Re Diplock*. "Or" is normally used disjunctively, in order to indicate the possibility of choice between different things.

Unfortunately, when the House of Lords, in 1944, gave their final opinion on this matter, five years after the propriety of the executors' action had been questioned, the executors had already distributed most of the residue to 139 charities. Some charities, like the prudent virgins in the parable, had kept their lamps burning and had already spent their windfalls, either in paying off mortgages, or in building extensions of their premises. Others, however, had left the sums received, either in their general funds, or in a special account. The next step taken by the next-of-kin was to call on the executors to make good the loss out of their own pockets—a stern reminder of the risks which a person runs gratuitously when he agrees to act as an executor or trustee. The executors made good a substantial portion of the loss in a compromise approved by the Court, but they were unable to refund in full. The second action entitled *Re Diplock* was therefore initiated with the object of compelling the charities to refund the sums which they had received without being entitled to them, and the problem to be resolved was whether there existed any legal or equitable principle which would compel the institutions which had been wrongly paid to refund. The extremely interesting answers to this problem given by Wynn-Parry, J., and the Court of Appeal and the House of Lords are discussed in Chapter IX; but the whole of this litigation is a salutary reminder that the task of the draftsman who is asked to give legal effect to the wishes of one who

[1] *Chichester Diocesan Fund and Board of Finance* v. *Simpson*.

desires to benefit charitable institutions is beset with pitfalls, and it seems to indicate that the penalties of a trifling slip, in putting "charitable *or* benevolent institutions", instead of "charitable *and* benevolent institutions" are excessive. Most of us would agree that that branch of the law which purports to define a charitable purpose is in an unsatisfactory state. The difficulty is to suggest better definitions than those which have so far been attempted.

As is well known, the starting-point of modern considerations of what constitutes a charitable purpose is Lord Macnaghten's definition in *Commissioners of Income Tax* v. *Pemsel*. In that case, he says: " 'Charity' in its legal sense comprises four principal divisions; trusts for the relief of poverty; trusts for the advancement of education; trusts for the advancement of religion; and trusts for other purposes beneficial to the community, not falling under any of the preceding heads."

And on the fourth head, he comments, "The trusts last referred to are not the less charitable in the eye of the law, because incidentally they benefit the rich as well as the poor, as, indeed, every charity that deserves the name must do either directly or indirectly."

A moment's reflection will lead to the conclusion that this so-called definition (the term is not Lord Macnaghten's) is not really a definition at all, but a classification. "Relief of poverty," "advancement of education," and "advancement of religion" are all exceedingly vague terms, which require a good deal of elucidation before they can be of service to the lawyer who is advising, or the judge who is deciding. And what are we to make of the fourth head of "other purposes beneficial to the community" especially when the decisions have long ago established the proposition that there is a wide class of purposes beneficial to the community, (or generally considered so) which are certainly not charitable? For example, if we are to accept the judgment of social historians, that progress is beneficial to the community, then we must concede that in modern times, with the development of parliamentary government, social progress has normally been secured by social legislation. Nevertheless, in *National*

Anti-Vivisection Society v. *Inland Revenue Commissioners* the majority of the House of Lords adopted an extract from Lord Parker's speech in *Bowman* v. *The Secular Society, Ltd.*, in which he said—

> Now if your lordships will refer for a moment to the society's memorandum of association you will find that none of its objects except possibly the first are charitable. The abolition of religious tests, the disestablishment of the Church, the secularisation of education, the alteration of the law touching religion or marriage, or the observation of the sabbath, are purely political objects. Equity has always refused to recognise such objects as charitable. It is true that a gift to an association formed for their attainment may, if the association be unincorporated, be upheld as an absolute gift to its members, or if the association be incorporated, as an absolute gift to the corporate body, but a trust for the attainment of political objects has always been held to be invalid, not because it is illegal, for every one is at liberty to advocate or promote by any lawful means a change in the law, but because the Court has no means of judging whether a proposed change in the law will or will not be for the public benefit, and therefore cannot say that a gift to secure the change is a charitable gift.

Accordingly, in the more recent case, the House of Lords took refuge behind the proposition (stated in *Thyssen on Charitable Bequests*) that "the law cannot stultify itself by holding that it is for the public benefit that the law itself shall be changed"—a somewhat strange doctrine for the mid-twentieth century.

In the *National Anti-Vivisection Society's* case, the House of Lords, overruling an earlier decision, *Re Foveaux*, held that a society advocating a change in the law to abolish vivisection, was not a charitable organisation. Previously, the law of charities had adopted the peculiarly liberal point of view that a society to promote vivisection was good as a charity, on the ground that it promoted medical education; and that a society advocating the suppression of vivisection was also charitable, since its object was to promote kindness to animals which, in other contexts, is regarded as a charitable purpose. *Re Foveaux*, however, was decided over fifty years ago, and Lord Wright gave a clear clue to the changed attitude of the courts today when he said, "To my mind the scale of the anti-vivisectionist mounts up and kicks the beam. The statesman is constantly weighing conflicting moral and material utilities."

That observation goes to the root of the matter. The solution of the problem whether a purpose is charitable or not is really a branch of public policy, for the result of deciding that a purpose is charitable is to place it within a favoured class, from which act it will normally derive substantial financial benefits. For example, in *Re Hummeltenberg*, decided in 1923, Russell, J., held that a project for the establishment of a college for the training of spiritualist mediums could not be regarded as charitable. Who shall say whether this decision will always stand? The discouraging effect of the decision upon the training of spiritualist mediums has been considerable, however.

Thus, the judge, in deciding charity cases is really making a decision, often of great importance, upon the trend of public policy. He indicates the channels into which private philanthropy can be directed with the greatest effect. In form he may appear to follow earlier decisions, but except where the terms of a later gift are identical with that of a gift in a reported case, his margin of freedom is wide, and it is impossible to exclude the personal factor in the choice between competing analogies. That is why, except in cases where a decision on an identical gift already exists, it is often almost impossible for a draftsman to predict whether the gift will take effect or not. Two striking illustrations of this are *Karen Kayemeth le Jisroel Ltd.* v. *Inland Revenue Commissioners*, (the "Jewish National Home" Case), and the more recent decision in *Williams' Trustees* v. *Inland Revenue Commissioners*, in which it was held that a fund for the purpose of maintaining a Welsh institute in London "for promoting the moral, social, spiritual and educational welfare of Welsh people" was non-charitable, as the community to which it was applicable was a fluctuating one.

How subjective the test applicable may be is shown by the conflicting decisions of English and Irish courts on gifts to closed orders of nuns. The law of charities in Ireland has been developed by judicial precedents from the same source as our own, yet the Irish courts have held that gifts to such closed orders are good,[1] and the English courts have held them to be bad.[2] Is that difference entirely unconnected with the fact that the predominant religion in Southern Ireland is Roman Catholicism, whilst in England the established religion is Protestantism?

In deciding that a purpose can properly be regarded as charitable, the Court is not making a decision which is binding in perpetuity, for the law of charities has developed its own safety valve. "If," said Lord Simonds in the *National Anti-Vivisection Society* case, "by a change in social habits and needs, or, it may be by a change in the law, the purpose of an established charity becomes superfluous or even illegal, or if, with increasing knowledge, it appears that a purpose once thought beneficial is truly detrimental to the community, it is the duty of trustees of an established charity to apply to the courts, or in suitable cases, to the Charity Commissioners, or, in educational charities, to the Minister of Education, and ask that a *cy-près* scheme may be established. A charity once established does not die, though its nature may be changed. But it is wholly consistent with this, that in a later age the Court should decline to regard as charitable a purpose, to which in an earlier age that quality would have been ascribed".

Here, it will be seen, the social implications of charity decisions are very clearly recognised. Nevertheless, it is difficult, if not indeed impossible, to discover the general conception of social policy on which the decisions are based. This difficulty is very clearly expressed by Lord Sterndale, M.R., in *Re Tetley*, where he says—

> I am unable to find any principle which will guide one easily, and safely, through the tangle of the cases as to what is and what is not a charitable gift. If it is possible I hope sincerely that at some time or other a principle will be laid down. The whole subject is in an artificial atmosphere altogether. A large number of gifts are held charitable which would not be called charitable in the ordinary acceptation of the term, and when one takes gifts which have been held to be charitable, and compares them with gifts which have

[1] *McNamee* v. *Mansfield*. [2] *Re Coats' Trusts*.

been held not to be charitable, it is very difficult to see what the principle is on which the distinction rests.

Like many other things in equity, the conception of a charitable purpose, such as it is today, is explicable only in the light of its history. All modern discussions of this question take as their starting-point the Statute of Charitable Uses of 1601, which gives the following enumeration of charitable purposes: "The relief of aged, impotent and poor people; the maintenance of sick and maimed soldiers and mariners; schools of learning, free schools, and scholars of universities; the repair of bridges, ports, havens, causeways, churches, seabanks and highways; the education and preferment of orphans; the relief, stock or maintenance of houses of correction; the marriage of poor maids; the supportation, aid and help of young tradesmen, handicraftsmen and persons decayed; the relief and redemption of prisoners and captives; the aid or ease of any poor inhabitants concerning payment of taxes."

This is a rather odd collection. It is manifestly not a definition at all, but an enumeration of a number of the more important charitable purposes at the time when the Act was passed, and it is in this way that it has always been regarded by the courts, for many of the purposes held good in recent times under Lord Macnaghten's fourth head can only be remotely associated with the objects specified in the statute. Where, for example, can one perceive in these objects an analogy with a gift of a sum of money to promote chess-playing among young persons in a specified town—a purpose which was held to be charitable in *Re Dupree's Trusts*, or with children's rides on elephants which, as educational, were regarded as charitable purposes by Farwell, J., in *Re Lopes*? Moreover, it should be noticed that certain assumptions underlie the list of 1601. This list includes "the repair of bridges, ports, havens, causeways and seabanks," yet a gift of money for the repair of a bridge or seabank on a private estate, or (for that matter) for a private road, has never been regarded as charitable. The element of public benefit was present as much in 1601 as it is today. Incidentally, it should be noticed that such objects as these, which were of great importance in 1601, are not nearly so important today, and might not necessarily be regarded as charitable objects at all. Social conditions have changed, and objects that were left to private philanthropy at the end of Elizabeth's reign are today major public services, for which the resources of local or national taxation are available. Today there would be many interesting things to be said upon the question whether a gift to the Railway Executive for the repair of Southampton Docks is still charitable.

So far as I know, the relation between the Statute of Charitable Uses of 1601, and contemporary social conditions has never been fully explored, although, as one would expect, Holdsworth has supplied us with valuable clues. He points out that this statute must be closely linked with our first great Poor Law, passed in the same year, and with still another Act passed in the same year, for the relief of soldiers and sailors by means of weekly pensions determined by Quarter Sessions, and paid out of a weekly rate levied on the parishes. These Acts were the consequences of the important economic changes of the sixteenth century, and they were evoked by a new conception of social responsibility. In the words of a high authority, they were "part of a paternal system of government under which the rulers regarded the maintenance of the usual prosperity of every class as part of their duties."[1] This involved the encouragement and regulation of charitable gifts from which the community in general, and especially the poorer members of it, could benefit.

There were, however, additional reasons peculiar to the law of charities, for the existence of the Statute of Charitable Uses. If the objects of the statute are examined in detail, it will be seen that they can for the most part be divided into the following four classes—

(1) *The relief of sick and maimed soldiers and sailors*, to which should be added the redemption of prisoners and captives. This was a matter of national concern at the end of Elizabeth's reign, for the long war on land and sea with Spain was ending, and numbers of destitute and maimed soldiers and sailors were crowding into the ports and towns. In an age

[1] Leonard, *Early History of Poor Relief*, p. 203.

when the first hesitant steps towards a national poor law system were being taken, the existence of this potentially turbulent class was a matter of general concern. The relief and redemption of prisoners and captives does not refer to persons lying in English jails for unpaid fines and debts, but to those unfortunates who had been captured abroad or on the high seas by non-Christian pirates, and whose release from slavery in the galleys or ashore on the North African coast could be secured by payment of ransom.

(2) *The relief of deserving poverty*, mainly in an urban setting. The Tudor period, and particularly Elizabeth's long reign, saw the increase of poverty on what was, for those times, an alarming scale. This was due to two distinct causes. The first was a change in the methods of agriculture, and an extension of sheep-farming, leading to the loss of employment by many agricultural labourers. These drifted into the towns, and in many cases became a charge on municipal funds. It was this class of poverty which was adversely affected by the suppression of the monasteries, for although the extent of the relief afforded by them can be exaggerated, it is nevertheless true that the monasteries gave a good deal of casual employment, and some of them ran something approximating to casual wards. The suppression of the monasteries therefore threw these rural unfortunates upon municipal relief, or in some cases, led to the formation of gangs of vagabonds, who terrorised the countryside. Altogether apart from this type of pauperism, there was another, urban in origin, which was due to the decay of the guilds, and the apprenticeship system which it regulated. Elizabeth's reign showed this decay far advanced, and its progressive replacement by individualist enterprise, employing labour hired for a wage, and uncertain in duration. Moreover, with the decay of the guilds, there collapsed a system of municipal philanthropy, which had not only reduced urban pauperism to small proportions, but had also contributed largely to municipal education, in the foundation of grammar schools, to municipal planning, in the construction of civic roads and buildings; and even to municipal religion, for the guilds had played a prominent part in the erection of some of the largest and most beautiful of

England's parish churches. It is for this reason that the list in the statute emphasises such objects as the building and maintenance of schools, the repair of municipal roads and buildings, the education of orphans, the marriage of poor maids, and " the supportation and help of young tradesmen handicraftsmen and persons decayed." One other purpose requires a word of explanation—"the relief, stock, or maintenance of houses of correction." These were the poorhouses of the period, to which the magistrates would consign idle and destitute vagabonds. At the end of Elizabeth's reign they were full to overflowing, and their maintenance was a problem which the Statute of Charitable Uses and the Poor Law Act of 1601 attempted to solve, with only partial success.

(3) *The advancement of education.* This object is implicit in the maintenance of schools, and scholars of universities, and, in another environment in "the education and preferment of orphans." At this date, it was already well understood that the advancement of all kinds of education was a charitable purpose, deserving of encouragement by private philanthropy, and the existence of the colleges of Oxford and Cambridge, of such great schools as Eton and Winchester, and of a surprisingly large number of local grammar schools (in which many of the greatest Elizabethans, for example, Shakespeare, Drake and Hawkins, were educated) sufficiently testified. The Oxford and Cambridge colleges and the great schools are recognised as charitable by Sect. 2 of the statute, but they are exempted from the system of control created by it because no special problems in respect of these had been created by the social and economic changes of the sixteenth century.

(4) *The advancement of religion.* On this head, the statute is almost completely silent, and the only reference to it is in the inclusion of churches in a list of buildings, the repair of which is charitable.[1] This, at first sight represents a wide change from medieval practice, for at that time the entire activities of the church, whether in the promotion of religion, or in the building of cathedrals, monasteries and chantries, had been

[1] In medieval times, the repair of churches in towns was often undertaken by the Guilds.

recognised as charitable. Indeed, they were "pious uses", and as Lord Eldon pointed out in *Moggridge* v. *Thackwell*, "we all know there was a period when, in this country, a portion of the residue of every man's estate was applied to charity," and until the Reformation this usually meant for the advancement of religion. It is in the existence of this former rule of English law that the origin of the *cy-près* doctrine is to be traced. It was customary for a person to indicate specific charitable purposes to be benefited, and if it was impossible to satisfy the wishes of the deceased, the next nearest object must be found. But the last thing that the Elizabethan legislator wanted was the intervention of private philanthropy in such a troubled question. The monasteries had been suppressed by Henry VIII, and the chantries by his son, Edward VI, who had also legislated against a return of Roman Catholicism under the head of "superstitious uses." Elizabeth, with infinite difficulty, had re-established a national Church, hanging both Roman Catholics and Anabaptists in the process. If, therefore, a man gave property to any religion other than that professed by the Anglican Church, he not only did not advance a charitable purpose, but he also broke the law of the land; in addition, he exposed himself to proceedings in the ecclesiastical courts for heresy. It was only when, in the eighteenth and nineteenth centuries, the attempt to establish uniformity of religious belief had been finally abandoned, and the disabilities on dissenters, non-Christians and Roman Catholics were progressively removed, that the courts, interpreting (as they claimed) the spirit of the Act of 1601, gradually admitted the advancement of these religions into a class of charitable objects. For all that, the Roman Catholic practice of "celebrating masses for the dead", was recognised as an infringement of the Statute of Superstitious Uses before the decision of the House of Lords in *Bourne* v. *Keane* in 1919, and it was not until 1934 that the practice was recognised as a charitable purpose in *Re Caus*. Even today (it has already been shown) a gift for a closed order of nuns is not charitable here, although it is in Ireland; nor would a gift for the advancement of spiritualism be regarded as charitable. In all probability, we have already passed the highwater mark of freedom to dispose of money for religious purposes, and at the same time to claim for these gifts recognition as charities. The nineteenth century decisions admitted some strange beliefs to the status of religion—for example, those of Joanna Southcote in *Thornton* v. *Howe*, decided in 1862. To indicate how far this decision goes, it is sufficient to quote the following extract from the Master of the Rolls' decision—

> The bequest is to propagate the sacred writings of Joanna Southcote. She, from her writings, was a very sincere Christian; but she laboured under the delusion that she would be made the medium of a miraculous birth of a child at an advanced period of her life, and that thereby the advancement of the Christian religion on earth would be promoted. But her works, as far as I have looked at them, contain but little upon this subject, and nothing which could shake the faith of any sincere Christian. In truth, though her works are in a great measure incoherent and confused, they are written obviously with a view to extend the influence of Christianity; and I cannot say that the bequest of a testator to publish and propagate works in support of the Christian religion is a charitable bequest, and at the same time say that if the testator should select for this purpose some three or four authors whose works will produce that effect, such a bequest thereupon ceases to be charitable; neither can I do so if a testator should select one single author whose works he thinks will produce that result. If a testator were to leave a fund for the purpose of propagating at a very reduced price the religious writings of Dr. Paley or Dr. Butler, I should be of opinion that the bequest was charitable in its character. I must hold the same in respect of what the testatrix has called the sacred writings of Joanna Southcote.

There spoke a great apostle of toleration in an age of intellectual freedom. If today, however, the courts should appear a little more hesitant in their approach to this question, it is not because of a weakening of the principle of toleration, but rather because the judge today is more conscious of another element in the problem—the element of social benefit. Planning, that is to say, may eventually intrude into the law of charities. Yet at this point it may be well to remember a word of warning from that great master of equity, Lord Eldon, who once observed that if testators were not assured that the objects of their bounty would receive their gifts, they would be in danger of omitting charitable bequests from their wills altogether.

Today, it is not often gifts for religious purposes which create problems, but gifts for political objects. In spite of the decision in *Re Scrowcroft*, it is now clear that a gift for the advancement of the work of a political party is not charitable, although it is surprisingly difficult to find this principle clearly formulated in the decisions. Even educational work of a serious nature in connection with the party's objects falls under the ban, as the decision in *Bonar Law Memorial Trusts* v. *Inland Revenue Commissioners*[1] shows. We may congratulate ourselves upon the wisdom shown by the courts in handling this delicate question, and in the attitude of neutrality which they have adopted, whilst recognising that increasingly difficult marginal cases are likely to occur from time to time. On the other hand, the suggestion in the recent decision of the House of Lords in *National Anti-Vivisection Society* v. *Inland Revenue Commissioners* that the advocacy of any legislative change cannot be a charitable purpose, may in the long run prove to be too precipitate a retreat from this field.

It will be seen that this chapter has so far sought to place the rules and decisions relating to charitable purposes in their historical and social setting, but it has not so far attempted to say what a "charitable purpose" is. It has been suggested that the decision whether a gift is charitable or not is really a decision on one head of public policy; and it has also been shown that such decisions involve a consideration of social benefit. Putting the matter in terms recognisable by the Chancery practitioner, we may say that all charitable gifts are "beneficial to the community," but as Lord Cave said in *A.G.* v. *National Provincial Bank*—

> Lord Macnaghten did not mean that all trusts beneficial to the community are charitable, but that there are certain charitable trusts which fall within that category; and therefore to argue that because a trust is for a purpose beneficial to the community it is therefore a charitable trust is to turn round his sentence and to give it a different meaning. So here it is not enough to say that the trust in question is for public

[1] See also *Re Hopkinson.*

purposes beneficial to the community or is for the public welfare; you must show it to be a charitable trust.

Observations such as these place the subject in an atmosphere of almost intolerable obscurity. They seem to imply—

(1) That all charitable trusts are beneficial to the community.

(2) That not all trusts beneficial to the community are charitable.

(3) That within the class of trusts beneficial to the community (i.e. public trusts) some independent criteria may be applied to determine whether a particular public trust is charitable or not.

Unfortunately, we are given only vague clues as to what those criteria may be, and where the gift cannot be assigned to one of the three wide classes: "advancement of religion," "advancement of education," and "relief of poverty," the determining criterion is the definition of Lord Macnaghten's fourth class, i.e. "those trusts beneficial to the community, but not falling under any of the other three heads." So that this process of definition is completely circular in operation.

Mr. Brunyate,[1] deriving some encouragement from a classification of charities included in the War Damage Act, 1943, Sect. 69, suggests a classification of charitable purposes under the following heads—

(1) The relief of poverty or other distress.

(2) The advancement of education, learning, science and research.

(3) The public advancement of religion.

(4) Purposes beneficial to the community not falling withn the preceding heads, which satisfy the following rules—

(*a*) A purpose is not charitable unless the benefit thereby conferred to the community is substantial having regard to the nature of what is given.

(*b*) A purpose which is for the direct benefit of a particular class of persons (other than a State institution) is not charitable, although it results in an indirect benefit to the community.

[1] *The Legal Definition of a Charity*, (1945), 61, *Law Quarterly Review*, pp. 268–85.

(*c*) Subject as aforesaid a purpose is charitable if either—
- (i) it confers a direct and tangible benefit on all members of the community; or
- (ii) it confers a direct and tangible benefit on a particular institution of the State tending to increase the efficiency of its communal activity; or
- (iii) not being for the direct benefit of a particular class of persons it is in the general enlightened opinion of the time wholly for the benefit of the community although such benefit be intangible.

(*d*) In this context the community means either the international community, the national community, or a local community (that is to say, a substantial geographical section of the national community) or a section of such a community determined by sex or age. Any other section of the community is to be regarded as a particular class of persons.

Mr. Brunyate himself adds immediately afterwards that his definition "may appear at first sight not to add much to Lord Macnaghten's," and I would respectfully agree with him. His definition appears to me to bristle with unsolved difficulties. How, for example, are we to determine whether a benefit is "substantial" or not. For example, would the benefit conferred in *Re Dupree's Trusts* (the chess-playing case) be considered substantial? And by what tests do you decide what is meant by "beneficial" (a difficulty which already exists)? For example, I was once asked whether a gift to a clinic for the extension of a knowledge of birth control could be regarded as charitable. And how would Joanna Southcote's writings (or Dr. Paley's) fare today under such a definition?

Again, what is meant by a "direct and tangible benefit"? This appears to be a big question. Or is it simply another way of saying "direct pecuniary benefit"? And I think most judges would be dismayed by the task of applying the language of (*c*) (iii).

My own solution of the conundrum is a more restricted one.

I do not think there is any comfort to be gained from definitions in this branch of the law. We must rely, as heretofore, upon the social acumen of the judges; but at the same time we are entitled perhaps to ask for a little more boldness in the formulation of principles. This is a branch of the law in which precedents lose their cogency through a change in social conditions, and in which analogies are frequently remote. Accordingly, I would ask for a periodic statement, preferably by the House of Lords, of some of the general principles upon which their charity decisions are founded, and for a reduction of the disastrous effects of decisions such as *Re Diplock*. Where an obvious technical slip such as this has been made, I would ask for power for the Court to direct the application of the fund exclusively for charitable purposes. But I should regard with apprehension any attempt to confine the development of the law of charities within the limits of a statutory definition.

In a review of the most significant developments in the law of torts during the past twenty-five years, a distinguished Canadian authority says: "The most important trend in the modern law of torts is the attempt to seek broad generalisations under which the facts of individual instances can be related, not with a view towards automatic solution, but rather with a view to the object or purpose to be attained."[1]

It is the reflection of a similar attitude in the law relating to charities, rather than complicated definitions and technical subtleties, which is urgently required at the present time.

[1] C. A. Wright, "The Law of Torts," in (1947), 25 *Canadian Bar Review*, p. 75.

CHAPTER VIII

The Nathan Report and Charities

The Report of the Nathan Committee on the Law and Practice relating to Charitable Trusts[1] was presented to Parliament in December, 1952, but unfortunately, with the exception of one small piece of legislation on a very special topic—the validation of some trusts as charitable which were limited for charitable and non-charitable purposes, and which took effect before December, 1952[2]—there have as yet been no consequences of the report by way of modification of the law. In particular, one important recommendation, which went a little beyond the law of charities and which extended to trusts generally—that trustees should have freedom to invest funds outside the present trustee range, which has already been discussed, has been ignored.

Meanwhile, the law of charities remains cumbrous, over-technical and in places (e.g. in the provisions relating to mortmain) anachronistic. There will be few who will dissent from the views expressed in paragraph 668—

> The first thing to be done is to shorten and simplify the law of charitable trusts: if there was one point on which witnesses were agreed it was this. We ourselves attach great importance to it, the more so because the vast majority of the people responsible for administering trusts are laymen giving their time and service voluntarily and without ready access to skilled professional assistance. It is a curious circumstance that, whereas in the matter of company law—a field in which, perhaps above all others, expert advice of all kinds is readily available—the legislature has thought fit to keep the law as intelligible as may be by passing consolidating Acts no less

[1] Cmd. 8710.

[2] The Charitable Trusts (Validation) Act, 1954, based on Chapter 12 of the Report.

than three times in the present century, the trustees of charitable trusts are expected to find their way through a tangle of statutes scattered over the last hundred years.

The reasons for the establishment of the Nathan Committee were social, rather than legal ones. The rapid social changes which have followed the war of 1939–45, and in particular, continuing and accelerating inflation, have generated the fear that private donation to charitable objects may be diminished in volume and effectiveness, and further, because many charities are tied to the statutory range of trustee investments, the funds available for the achievement of charitable objects may become increasingly inadequate for this purpose. Moreover, in an age of rapid social change, it was only to be expected that the rigidity of the *cy-près* doctrine, confined as it has been by the courts within narrow limits, should be felt to be a restriction on the work of charitable organisations. This, indeed, had been stressed by Lord Beveridge in his book *Voluntary Action: A Report on Methods of Social Advance*, published in 1948. Besides these major questions, there are a number of related ones. Any survey of the law of charities with the object of reforming it must grapple with the vexed question of definition, which has already been discussed.[1] Further a large charitable organisation, administering many charitable trusts finds the necessity to appropriate investments to each charitable activity increasingly irksome and time-consuming, yet until recent years the courts have always insisted that such specific appropriations, and separate accounting, must be maintained in respect of each charitable fund, no matter how small. Recently, however, there have been signs of a change of attitude, for Vaisey, J., held in *Re Royal Society's Charitable Trusts*, that the Court was prepared to sanction proposals by trustees, where the Attorney-General raised no objection, to consolidate the trust funds into one common pool, in which the several trusts are to be regarded as interested in appropriate shares, and also to permit the enlargement of the range of investments for such a combined fund. Once again the Court declined to regard this authorisation as being within the terms of Sect. 57 of the

[1] *Ante* Chapter VI.

Trustee Act, 1925, or within its inherent general jurisdiction. Vaisey, J., preferred to put it on the ground that, where the Attorney-General consents or does not object, the Court is in fact authorising such proposals in respect of a scheme, and Vaisey, J., was careful to add—

> This is, however, in my view, an exceptional case. There is evidence that the Royal Society takes special care in selecting and varying its investments. Again, it by no means follows that the range of investment ought to be widened as of course whenever a charity finds its available income less than the trustees of it would wish. The existence of a multiplicity of trusts under the administration of one trustee ought not in every case to be regarded as justifying a pooling of investments. The jurisdiction which I hold that I have, should, in my judgment, be exercised sparingly, and not indiscriminately.

Nevertheless the door is at long last ajar, but by way of judicial decision, not by legislation.

The overriding purpose of the Nathan Report was to study the law of charities from the standpoint of its social purpose, and to demonstrate the continuing need for voluntary action in the welfare state. Some former charitable purposes—for example, hospitals—since 1945 have become part of the State's national health system. There was nothing particularly novel in this, for at an earlier period the provision of education had been largely left to voluntary charitable activity, which, from 1870, was largely superseded by a national system for which the State assumed responsibility. Today, even the universities, though private in form, depend to a substantial and increasing degree upon State-aid, even though there is still scope for charitable endowment of them.

In Chapter 1 of the Report, the Committee traces the development of charitable activity through the centuries. It pays a well-merited tribute to the great effort of the medieval church to provide universal relief for the necessities of men by appeals to the virtue of Christian charity, and it stresses the disorganisation which was brought about in the sixteenth century as a result of the Reformation. This disorganisation produced, on the one side, a national system of poor relief, and on the other, the Statute of Charitable Uses of 1601. The first contemplated State action, the second was designed to encourage voluntary activity, and the two were regarded as complementary. "Indeed," the Report adds, "historically, State action is voluntary action crystallised and made universal." This is true, not only of poor relief, but also of education, and provision of hospital services at a much later date.

These later manifestations of the charitable impulse, the Report points out, were part of a great nineteenth century humanitarian movement, which served as a corrective to the harsher implications of *laissez-faire*. Once again, this strong impulse led, on the one side, to the growth of local government, to progressive extensions of the franchise, and finally to the development by the State of a succession of positive functions which, in our own day, have culminated in the welfare state. On the other hand, the same impulse has led to an immense increase in the number of voluntary organisations of all kinds, devoted to social welfare, in the broadest sense of the term. Often, too, voluntary activity has preceded, and made possible, state intervention at a later date. Not all of these, it may be added, qualify as charities in the legal sense, although in some cases, this is rather the accident of judicial precedent than conscious design, and if, as has already been suggested, the task of framing a comprehensive definition of a charitable purpose is an impossible task, it might well be that there would be considerable benefit to be derived from regarding as a charity those objects which fall within the principles of socially valuable activity which are discussed in general terms in Chapter I of the Nathan Report. The Nathan Report itself speaks somewhat uncertainly upon the question of definition, and eventually all the members of the Committee except Mr. H. E. Salt reached the conclusion that the best way to face the problem would be to give statutory form to Lord Macnaghten's classification in *Pemsel's* case. It is, however, a little difficult to see what would be gained by this. Ever since the *Pemsel* case, Chancery judges have habitually cited and followed Lord Macnaghten's classification, and to embody it in statutory form would scarcely give the judges that greater freedom of decision which the Committee would like to see.[1]

[1] Para. 139, p. 36.

Chapter II of the Report contains a most valuable concise history of the law and practice of charitable trusts.

"The Ecclesiastical Courts (it observes), in effect, conferred three related privileges on charitable trusts and only on charitable trusts: the privilege of exemption from the rule against perpetuities; the privilege of being a valid or 'good' trust even if the testamentary disposition to charity was in imprecise terms (in which case precise terms would be laid down by the Court); and the privilege of obtaining fresh objects if those laid down by the founder were at the outset, or became, incapable of execution. So long as a gift to charity manifested a 'general charitable intention' that was sufficient to make it good. The precise terms considered essential to make good other dispositions were not required to make good a gift to charity. This principle was taken very far. Indeed in the absence of express directions in wills it was understood that the residue should be expended on pious and charitable works. . . .

"The doctrine of *cy-près* was developed in order that these three related privileges might not be defeated. It is essentially a device for keeping in existence a gift to charity so that it may continue as a public benefit from generation to generation. Its limitations arise from the principle that the donor's or testator's wishes must be respected and must not be disregarded even though the endowment created by him could clearly be put to better use."[1]

From 1597 onwards, the legislature made repeated attempts to control and eradicate abuses in the administration of charities. The statute of 1601 was itself an important attempt to achieve this by providing that Commissioners to enquire into abuses should be appointed from time to time. Such appointments ceased in the eighteenth century, and in the nineteenth century the problem was tackled afresh. All earlier efforts to control charities were superseded by the Charitable Trusts Act, 1853, which established the Charity Commissioners, as well as the Official Trustee of Charity Lands and the Official Trustees of Charitable Funds. The establishment of these last two offices provided a means whereby both land

[1] Report, pp. 16–17.

and personal property could be held by public corporations at no cost to the trustees, and without any interference with the administration of the trust, and the Nathan Committee suggested that all lands and investments of charities should be vested in them.[1]

Later Acts extended the powers of the Charity Commissioners. In particular the Act of 1860 gave them powers concurrent with those of the Chancery Division to establish or modify schemes, subject to an appeal to the Court. This power, however, like that possessed by the Court, could be exercised in relation to the modification of charitable schemes only within the limits of the *cy-près* doctrine.

Coincidently with the demand for a more effective system of control for charities, there was a demand for a relaxation of the rigidity of the *cy-près* doctrine. As far as charities in general were concerned, the demand was unsuccessful, but in so far as educational trusts were concerned, the Endowed Schools Act, 1869, gave power to an independent commission to reorganise educational trusts within its jurisdiction "in such manner as may render them most conducive to the advancement of education of boys and girls or either of them." These powers were transferred to the Board of Education in 1899 and are now vested in the Minister of Education.

It is easy to overlook the fact that reformers of a century ago were contending for changes in the law of charity which are considered to be as desirable today as they were a century ago, and that the body of reformist opinion was probably more influential then than it is now. The Report sums up the present state of the problem in three paragraphs—

> 103. There are now some 110,000 charitable trusts known to the Commissioners and the Ministry. Of these, 30,000 are educational, practically all of which are subject to the wider scheme-making powers of the Endowed Schools Act of 1869. But the remaining 80,000 are still subject to the strict *cy-près* doctrine. There are no up-to-date statistics on how these 80,000 trusts are divided between those for the advancement of religion and those for the relief of poverty or those for other charitable purposes within the Commissioners' jurisdiction.

[1] Report, pp. 56–57.

But we may hazard a guess, on the strength of statistics prepared by the Commissioners in 1876 and on the (possibly big) assumption that the proportion of income held by the various classes of trusts will not have changed materially since then, that well over half are trusts appropriated to the poor or to the sick in one form or another in doles of money and gifts in kind, almshouses, hospitals and so on. All these have been affected in one way or another by the steadily rising standard of life in the last hundred years and by the social legislation of the last fifty years.

104. Hundreds, perhaps thousands, of trusts need revision, and to an extent that goes beyond anything that could be achieved under the present *cy-près* doctrine. Many trustees no doubt take a commonsense line and, stretching their trust purposes to the utmost, or perhaps even beyond their strict limits, manage to continue to put their trust funds to good use, but some may accumulate their funds against the hoped-for day when the *cy-près* doctrine is relaxed, and would enable the funds to be put to "the maximum benefit of the community"; yet others are unaware of the changed conditions of the day and may not have looked critically at their trust objects in the light of them. There are trusts, of course, with sufficiently wide objects to enable them to weather such changes and to set a new course for themselves without the need for a scheme, and many others which are unaffected by these changes. There can be no doubt, however, that the need for some relaxation of the *cy-près* doctrine, so long pressed, is extensive and has now become urgent.

105. We do not wish to conjure up a lurid picture of hundreds of freakish or archaic trusts crying out for reform, but rather of a vast number of trusts which may broadly be called "social welfare trusts" which are by no means useless but are not serving the community as they might if some relaxing of the *cy-près* doctrine were introduced, together with the administrative machinery to make it a reality. The trusts may be devoted to objects which are relatively well provided for elsewhere while others are crying out for more support; or the objects themselves may not be open to criticism but the beneficial area may need to be changed or enlarged; or the qualification of beneficiaries may need to be broadened if fuller use is to be made of these trusts.

A study of cases such as *Re Campden Charities* and *Re Dominion Students Hall* will show how a change in social conditions will be productive of embarrassment for trustees. In both of these cases *cy-près* modification was possible, but in *Re Weir Hospital* it was not, yet it is scarcely open to question that if in the latter case the scheme for the amalgamation of two inadequately-supported hospitals had been accepted, the problems of the trustees would have been diminished, and the public as a whole would have gained.

The Report contains some interesting proposals for the recording of charitable trusts. This is a problem of long standing, and it is, as the Committee state, astounding that no classified records of charitable trusts exist. In consequence, no-one knows how many charitable trusts there are, or what their resources are, or how their funds are distributed. This is possibly even more remarkable, when it is appreciated that registration of charities has been directed by more than one statute, and in particular, by the Charitable Donations Registration Act, 1813. The provisions of such acts, however, have quickly fallen into disuse. The Charity Commissioners are not required to compile statistics or to maintain a register. They are not even required to ensure that the objects and existence of charitable trusts are brought to the notice of those who are liable to benefit from them. The Committee therefore recommend that all charitable trustees should be required to send to the Charity Commissioners as to the Ministry of Education particulars of their trusts, and should be also required to make an annual return of any changes in their status. They also recommend that the Charity Commissioners and the Ministry should compile and keep complete classified records for themselves, and classified and up-to-date records of local trusts for local authorities, all such records to be open to public inspection. Unhappily, there is as yet no indication that this overdue improvement is likely to be put into force, nor has the suggestion of the Committee that the accounts of charitable trustees should be audited regularly, and that copies should be sent to the Charity Commissioners and the Ministry, been proceeded with. The absence of any such provision in the law is the more remarkable since one great voluntary organisation, the Football Association, has always required each of the 30,000 clubs under its jurisdiction to send annually audited copies of its accounts to the county association, or to the Football Association itself, and compliance with this requirement operates as a valuable check on administration, and produces few difficulties in practice.

As might have been expected, the Report comments adversely upon the over-technical condition of the present law relating to mortmain, and also upon the various technical formalities which, apart from mortmain, are necessary in the case of transfers of charity land. The Report, whilst accepting the retention of those restrictions which are framed to ensure that the Charity Commissioners or the Ministry retain control over transfers of charity land, considers that the mortmain and charitable uses restrictions are an anachronism and should be repealed, together with the recording of assurances under Sect. 29 (4) of the Settled Land Act, 1925, and Sect. 87 (2) of the Education Act, 1944.

The restrictions on conveyances into mortmain were of first importance in the Middle Ages, when the incidents of feudal tenure were still realities, and when there were major dangers in the progressive concentration of land, then the prime source of wealth, in the hands of the Church, but they are anachronisms in the twentieth century. With them should also disappear the last vestiges of the doctrine of "superstitious uses", which lost any significance it might then have had with the decision of the House of Lords in *Bourne* v. *Keane*.

Chapter 9 of the Report examines in detail the defects of the *cy-près* doctrine, and also Scottish legislation providing for the modification of educational trusts, which the Committee thought might well be applied to charitable trusts generally. Relaxation of the *cy-près* doctrine is, in fact, the key to a more rational law of charities, for it would make such of the over-technicality in the decisions on the question whether a particular object is charitable or not meaningless. The Nathan Committee suggested that the legislature should prescribe circumstances in which the obsolescence of charitable objects can be assumed. Alterations should not, however, be made within thirty-five years of the foundation of the trust without the consent of the trustees and the founder. Further, wherever alterations are made, special regard should be had to the spirit of the intention of the founders, the interest of the locality to which the endowment belongs, and the possibility of achieving administrative economy by merging endowments. There was a good deal of discussion by the Committee whether the proper authority to exercise the extended powers for changing schemes should be the Court or the Charity Commissioners, but the conclusion was eventually reached that the Commissioners or the Ministry should exercise them, although the existing powers of the Chancery Division in respect of schemes should be retained. The exercise of these wider powers by the Commissioners should, however, be subject to an appeal to the Court. The proposal to give the Commissioners these wider powers is not new, and indeed, the decisions show that upon occasion, the Commissioners have accepted rather bolder modification of schemes than the Court, under the existing law, was prepared to sanction.

One aspect of the law to which the Report gives considerable attention is the constitution and functions of the central authorities. These are discussed in Chapter 10, together with the position of charities exempt from the jurisdiction of the Charity Commissioners. Broadly speaking, the Report recommends that charities at present exempt from the jurisdiction of the Charity Commissioners or the Ministry should retain their present status, but that machinery should be set up for revising the schemes of trusts which they administer more freely than is the case at present. It is also recommended that all university bodies should have power to establish unified trust funds, where they do not at present enjoy such a power. Since the decision in *Re Royal Society's Charitable Trusts*, however, an advance is being made in this sphere independently of legislation. It is also recommended—

> (*h*) that a plain charity should be redefined in law as a charity whose property is in the nature of current or recurrent voluntary contributions any investments representing accumulations thereof, all of which are capable of being expended: and that a plain charity should be subject to the general powers of enquiry now contained in Sect. 9 of the Charitable Trusts Act, 1853, but should otherwise be excluded from the jurisdiction: that any member of the public should

have the right to draw the attention of the Commissioners or of the Ministry to any plain charity which *prima facie* requires investigation, and that the facilities offered by the Official Custodians[1] should be available to any plain charity wishing to take advantage of them;

(*i*) that all mixed charities as defined by us should record particulars of their purposes and all their assets and any changes in them; should be subject to the general powers of enquiry and should submit annual audited accounts; should vest their land and securities in the Official Custodians; should seek consent to dealings in land; but should be free to spend their non-endowed assets not being land or to have them schemed with their endowed property, as they think fit.

These proposals, if embodied in legislation, would clear up the legal obscurity which surrounds charities maintained by voluntary contributions and mixed charities,[2] whilst at the same time giving greater promise of more efficient administration. In particular, it would resolve some of the uncertainties which surround the sales of land of mixed charities, on which Mr. A. H. Withers has commented that the existence of such uncertainty was no credit to English law.[3]

Part III of the Report makes some important proposals relating to the organisation of charitable trusts, which are intended to ensure that they are of maximum benefit to the community. Upon some of these suggestions opinion may differ widely, and some of them may appear to the lawyer to be somewhat sweeping. For example, in Chapter 13, it is proposed that a number of the smallest trusts should be merged, and that others with an annual value of less than £100 might be put into a county unified trust fund to be run by a separate board of trustees chosen primarily for their financial experience and judgment. It is probable that this suggestion owes something to the spread of the "community chest" idea in the United States. A special chapter of the Report is devoted to parochial charities. These, where they are non-ecclesiastical are subject not only to the Charitable Trusts Acts but also to the Local Government Act, 1894. The

[1] Who are intended to replace the Official Trustees of Charity Lands and Investments with extended functions.

[2] On which see *Re Clergy Orphan Corporation.*

[3] *Sales of Lands of Mixed Charities* (Reprinted 1957).

Report proposed that the accounts of these charities should be audited and laid before the parish meeting or parish council. There should also be reviews of the work of these charities by the appropriate local authority. The Report also advocates the progressive establishment, following the American example, of Community Chests and Community Trusts. Common Good funds have long been established in Scotland, the trustees being the town council, and in recent years, there has been some extension of the idea to England, the best-known example being the Birmingham Common Good Trust.[1] The Report is clear, however, that the objects should be general in nature, local in operation, spontaneous in origin, and unofficial in character. Somewhat more cautiously, also, the Report expressed the view that there was scope for national common good trusts. They should be set up by statute, with trustees appointed by the Queen in Council. They should be equipped with a substantial annual income, and a further interesting suggestion is that *bona vacantia* should be transferred to them.

It will be apparent that the Nathan Committee presented a comprehensive plan for re-shaping the law of charities, as an instrument of social service. Some parts of the proposals, as for example the introduction of greater flexibility into the definition of a charity, the relaxation of the *cy-près* doctrine, the abolition of the doctrines of mortmain and superstitious uses may be regarded as non-controversial. Others, such as the extension of the administrative functions of the Commissioners, the audit of charity accounts and the registration of charities might be regarded as generally desirable, although there might be differences of opinion concerning the precise extent of the changes to be made. Other suggestions again, such as those advocating the merging of smaller charities and the setting up of national and local common good funds may raise questions of broad social policy. So far, there has been no indication that any substantial part of the Report will be implemented by legislation. Possibly this is because no Government Department is deeply concerned with the functioning of charities as a whole, although the Ministry of Education

[1] Report, p. 152.

now has a special responsibility in respect of educational charities. Accordingly, the law of charities remains unreformed, cumbrous, and in places exceedingly obscure. It ought not, however, to be beyond the reforming zeal of the mid-twentieth century to produce a comprehensive statute that will give this branch of the law a fresh start.

CHAPTER IX

The Diplock Case and the Underpaid Beneficiary

PERIODICALLY there arises in the Chancery Division a case of major importance, in which a considerable variety of equitable problems call for solution together. One example of this was the protracted litigation which arose out of Caleb Diplock's will, one portion of which, embodied in the first set of proceedings, culminating in *Chichester Diocesan Fund* v. *Simpson*, has already been discussed. As a result of that decision of the House of Lords, the residuary gift for "charitable or benevolent" purposes failed for uncertainty, so that the residue vested in the next-of-kin. Unfortunately, by the time this had been established, the residue had been almost completely distributed to over a hundred medical charities. There thus remained the problem of the recovery of the funds from those who were now found to have no title to them. The matter was still further complicated by the fact that, under the National Health Service Act, 1946, the property of the hospitals had vested in the Minister of Health. The lengthy proceedings directed to the recovery of this property was at length settled by the decision of the House of Lords in *Minister of Health* v. *Simpson*.

By a long established rule of equity, the first persons to be attacked in a situation such as this must be the unfortunate trustees themselves, who now found themselves liable to refund £250,000. This was, in the circumstances, quite impossible, and proceedings against them were compromised in exchange for a payment by them of approximately £60,000. Unfortunately, the strain of these proceedings proved fatal to one of the trustees. The next question was whether the next-of-kin had a claim against those institutions to whom the fund had been distributed, or rather, against the Minister of Health, as their successor in title. Still a further complication was that the hospitals had dealt with these windfalls in different ways. In one or two cases they still retained the funds. Others had used the funds to meet current expenses. Others again had added funds of their own to the gift and had built extensions to their hospitals.

It was established that the payments were made under a mistake of law. Equity, however, in a suitable case will relieve against a mistake of law. The next question to be decided was whether the next-of-kin had a right to follow the assets into the hands of a person receiving them wrongfully but in good faith. If this was conceded, had the next-of-kin an action *in rem*, by virtue of the doctrine of tracing (often termed the Rule in *Hallett's* case) and had they perhaps, some other, and wider remedy, i.e. an action *in personam*, independent of the doctrine of tracing, against the institutions themselves?

To these questions the House of Lords in *Ministry of Health* v. *Simpson* answered that the next-of-kin had the right to trace the assets against those who had wrongly received them, and that, in addition, they had a right *in personam* against the institutions themselves. In this, they were at one with the Court of Appeal.

In effect, the speech of Lord Simonds, L.C., was the speech of the entire House, for all the other Law Lords accepted it without modification. It is, in essence, a most acute re-examination and reaffirmation of the decision of the Court of Appeal, which varied the decision of Wynn-Parry, J., at first instance. Lord Simonds's speech begins with these very significant words, which have a direct bearing on the importance of legal research in legal practice—

> My Lords, I think that the reasoning and conclusion of the Court of Appeal are unimpeachable and it is right to add that, if Wynn-Parry, J., had had the advantage of the citation of authorities and of the argument based upon them which the Court of Appeal and your Lordships have had, he might have come to a different conclusion.

The full significance of that observation becomes apparent when the judgments in the courts below are studied. The report of the case in the Court of Appeal occupies exactly 100 pages in the Law Reports. The report of Wynn-Parry, J.'s, judgment is almost as lengthy. In the Court of Appeal the judgment was the judgment of the Court, in which all three members concurred. The two judgments illustrate at once the strength of the historical method and the necessity for an exhaustive examination of the sources of a legal rule. Wynn-Parry, J.'s, judgment is an exhaustive analysis of the cases from 1800 onwards. From this investigation, Wynn-Parry, J., concluded that the next-of-kin had no right *in personam* against the hospitals and that even the right *in rem* was very limited. The Court of Appeal, however, investigated the matter further. Again remarking that the question was one of great difficulty and complexity, they added—

> It has involved considerable research into cases over a period of more than two hundred and fifty years and we have been much indebted to counsel for the help which their industry and argument have given to this Court.

Such further investigation vindicated the existence of a right *in personam* which Wynn-Parry, J., on research over a shorter period, had been unable to recognise. The search back to the Restoration was in this case of first importance for, as Holdsworth points out in a passage cited by the Court of Appeal, this was exactly the period when the Court of Chancery was taking over jurisdiction from the ecclesiastical courts. As might be expected, therefore, the Court of Chancery was defining and explaining the rights enjoyed by personal representatives and legatees.

The right of the next-of-kin to trace as against the hospitals was treated somewhat differently by the three courts. In the very full discussion of this in Wynn-Parry, J.'s, judgment, he points out that "where a person other than the true owner thereof pays money into an account at his bank, and does not mix with that money any other money, either his own or that of any other person, the true owner of the money can at common law follow it into that account, and further can follow it out of the account into any asset or assets which can be shown to have been purchased wholly with it." He goes on to point out that this right at common law does not depend upon any fiduciary relationship, but is lost whenever the identity of the *res* is gone, and this takes place whenever other money is mixed with the fund to be recovered. Since *Hallett's* case, the equitable rule is wider, in that the Court there laid down rules for following the assets where the trustee had mixed trust money with his own money. On the other hand, the equitable remedy of tracing is available only where a fiduciary relationship exists. This, in the view of Wynn-Parry, J., was an insuperable obstacle in the *Diplock* case. There was no fiduciary relationship between the next-of-kin and the institutions to whom the estate had been wrongly distributed. The claim to trace therefore failed, wherever the recipients had mixed trust money with their own money. In cases where this had not taken place it might seem that the money could be recovered in virtue of the common law right, but even here, Wynn-Parry, J., held that once the money had been placed in the recipient's banking account, its identity was lost, and it did not revive even when the institutions subsequently earmarked the money received as "the Diplock fund." The common law remedy, in fact, was available only where the recipients had placed the Diplock money in a separate account from the outset. In such a case, provided it had not been mixed with other money, it could be reclaimed, even if it had been used to purchase other assets. In the latter case, the next-of-kin could claim the actual assets. Finally, Wynn-Parry, J., pointed out that wherever a recipient had paid money into a separate account and had not mixed it with other money, then after receiving notice of the next-of-kin's claim, the recipient became a trustee of the fund, and all the usual remedies of tracing would attach to the fund after the date of the warning.

The view taken by Wynn-Parry, J., of the extent of the application of the doctrine of tracing was in any event a somewhat narrow one. If it is restricted to cases where there is a clear trust relationship, then it is difficult to account for the decision of the House of Lords in *Sinclair* v. *Brougham.* It also excludes tracing from the decision of Warrington, J., in *Re Robinson.* Indeed, Wynn-Parry, J., says expressly of Warrington, J.'s, judgment—

> He examined the contention of the plaintiff that in regard to a mere money demand there was a claim in equity other

than a claim analogous to the common law action of money had and received, and in my judgment, so far from having by implication, admitted the existence of such a claim in equity, the learned judge, when his judgment is considered as a whole, negatived it.

The Court of Appeal took a much broader view of the doctrine of tracing. They held that *Sinclair* v. *Brougham* had shown that *Hallett's* case is simply an illustration of a much wider principle. This wider principle dispenses with the necessity for a fiduciary relationship in the true sense to exist between the parties. It is explained by Greene, M.R., delivering the judgment of the Court as follows—

> There is an equitable principle common to all these cases of mixed funds. It operates in different ways according to the circumstances. In some cases it results in a priority to one or other of the claimants, in other cases the claimants rank *pari passu*. Where one claimant is a person in a fiduciary relationship to another and has mixed moneys of that other with moneys of his own, that other takes priority. The same result follows where a person taking that other claimant's money from the person in a fiduciary relationship with notice that it is money held in a fiduciary capacity, proceeds to mix it with money of his own. When the contest is between two claimants to a mixed fund made up entirely of moneys held on behalf of the two of them respectively and mixed together by the fiduciary agent, they share *pari passu*, each being innocent. Where the moneys are handed by way of transfer to a person who takes for value without notice, the claim of the owner of the moneys is extinguished just as all other equitable estates or interests are extinguished by a purchase for value without notice. In the case, however, of a volunteer who takes without notice, e.g. by way of gift from the fiduciary agent, if there is no question of mixing, he holds the money on behalf of the true owner whose equitable right to the money still persists as against him. On the other hand, if the volunteer mixes the money with money of his own, or receives it mixed from the fiduciary agent, he must admit the claim of the true owner, but is not precluded from setting up his own claim in respect of the moneys of his own which have been contributed to the mixed fund. The result is that they share *pari passu*. It would be inequitable for the volunteer to claim priority for the reason that he is a volunteer: it would be equally inequitable for the true owner of the money to claim priority over the volunteer for the reason that the volunteer is innocent and

> cannot be said to act unconscionably if he claims equal treatment for himself. The mutual recognition of one another's rights is what equity insists upon as a condition of giving relief.

This equitable principle of tracing has been extended widely since it was formulated by Sir George Jessel in 1879. *Re Hallett's* case, *Sinclair* v. *Brougham*, and *Re Diplock*[1] are therefore no more than illustrations of it in differing circumstances.

This, however, is by no means the extent of the contribution of the *Diplock* case to equity. It had been argued before Wynn-Parry, J., that the next-of-kin had a right *in personam* to recover the funds wrongly distributed to the hospitals, independently of any question of tracing. Wynn-Parry, J., rejected this claim since, as has been mentioned, a review of the precedents down to 1800 failed to disclose it. Here again the Court of Appeal, on more extended research, reached a different conclusion.

In fact, as the Master of the Rolls pointed out, there were two distinct claims for a remedy *in personam*, both of which were rejected by Wynn-Parry, J. The first claim was that after the hospitals had received notice of the claim of the next-of-kin, they were subjected to a constructive trust of the moneys they had received. This, of course, would unquestionably be the case once a court of equity had decided that the next-of-kin's claim was well-founded, but before that time they had no duty towards him. They were, as the Court of Appeal held, entitled to assume that the executors were distributing the estate properly.

The second type of claim *in personam* raised the wider question of the rights of beneficiaries where an estate is being distributed, either under a will or on intestacy. Here Wynn-Parry, J., had held that an unpaid beneficiary could only sue *in personam* in the same circumstances as those which would enable him in the name of or by joining the personal representative to sue at law, i.e. when the wrong payment had been made under a mistake of fact. This, it has been mentioned, was all that the cases since *Gillespie* v. *Alexander* appeared to justify.

[1] Tracing was not discussed by the House of Lords.

The Court of Appeal agreed with Wynn-Parry, J., that the mistake was one of law, and not of fact. Nevertheless, they pointed out that the view taken by the learned judge did not account for the decisions of *David* v. *Frowd* and *Mohan* v. *Broughton*, nor for the statement in *Seton on Judgments and Orders*[1]: "Though the estate has been distributed among those found to be next-of-kin they are liable in general to refund to the real next-of-kin . . . and an action may be brought by such real next-of-kin for the purpose."

The Court of Appeal traced this action back to a series of decisions shortly after the Restoration, finding its origin in the desire of the Court of Chancery to give legatees and next-of-kin a general remedy which would make it unnecessary for them to resort to the spiritual court. The remedy, the Court of Appeal emphasises, was a general one. It did not depend upon whether the estate was being administered by the Court, and the early cases do not restrict it to mistakes of fact. Nor did it matter that the original recipient eventually turns out to be a stranger to the estate. The right is, however, subject to the qualification that the true beneficiary must first exhaust his remedy against the personal representatives, and his claim should be limited to the amount which he cannot recover from them. Further, it would seem that claims under this head are for the principal only, and not for any interest, whilst finally, the period of limitation applicable to these claims is twelve years under Sect. 20 of the Limitation Act, 1939.

In the House of Lords, only the claim *in personam* was discussed, and the House affirmed the opinion expressed by the Court of Appeal upon it. Lord Simonds, L.C., in his speech, however, points out that the right of the next-of-kin in this case is derived from the fact that there is an administration of assets. No similar right *in personam* is enjoyed by a beneficiary under a trust—unless, one might add, the Court at some similar date, should extend the principle, as it has extended the principle of tracing in the *Diplock* case.

Possibly the most interesting part of Lord Simonds's speech is that in which he emphatically repudiates the defence of

[1] 7th Ed., Vol. II, p. 1595.

mistake of law in cases of this kind. Dealing with the earlier cases, he says—

> In the first place, though in almost all the reported cases the probability is that the wrongful payment was made under a mistake of fact, that is not true of all of them and in many of them, while the probability is in one direction, there can be no certainty without further information which is not now available. This leads directly to the second reason. In not one of the many cases where the equity was applied was any suggestion made in argument or judgment that the issue depended on the nature of the mistake under which the wrongful payment had been made. It is not credible that, if the distinction between mistake of fact and law was relevant, it would never have been mentioned, particularly at a time when in the courts of common law it was being established. And here it may be observed that the equitable doctrine was well settled before that event took place. . . .
>
> In the third place the most satisfactory reason for the distinction rests in the maxim, itself probably taken from the criminal law. . . . The man who makes a wrong payment because he has mistaken the law may not plead his own ignorance of the law and so cannot recover what he has wrongfully paid. It is difficult to see what relevance this distinction can have, where a legatee does not plead his own mistake or his own ignorance but, having exhausted his remedy against the executor who has made the wrongful payment, seeks to recover money from him who has been wrongfully paid. To such a suit the executor was not a necessary party and there was no means by which the plaintiff could find out whether his mistake was of law or of fact or even whether his wrongful act was mistaken or deliberate. He could guess and ask the Court to guess but he could prove nothing. I reject therefore the suggestion that the equitable remedy in such circumstances was thus restricted and repeat that it would be a strange thing if the Court of Chancery, having taken upon itself to see that the assets of a deceased person were duly administered, was deterred from doing justice to the creditor, legatee or next-of-kin because the executor had done him wrong under a mistake of law. If in truth this were so, I think that the Father of Equity would not recognise his child.

The second *Diplock* case thus demonstrated the breadth and flexibility of the equitable remedy of tracing, and in addition it defined the extent of the personal right enjoyed by an underpaid beneficiary against any person who has obtained assets without title to them. Since, as has been shown, this right is enjoyed in virtue of the fact that it arises out of the administration of the estate of a deceased person, the *Diplock* case did not discuss whether a similar right should be enjoyed by a beneficiary under a trust. No similar body of precedents exists to help him, yet in view of the extensions of the remedy of tracing which have been made in *Sinclair* v. *Brougham* and the *Diplock* case, it should not be assumed that the Court will necessarily refuse to make a comparable extension in respect of the right *in personam* also.

TABLE OF CASES

Table of Cases

INDEX

Index